A LITTLE GIANT® BOOK

LAUGHS

A LITTLE GIANT® BOOK

LAUGHS

Matt Rissinger and Philip Yates

STERLING

New York / London
www.sterlingpublishing.com/kids

In memory of our longtime friend and editor,
Sheila Anne Barry

Library of Congress Cataloging-in-Publication Data Available

The Little Giant Book of Laughs / Matt Rissinger and Philip Yates.
   p. cm.
  Includes index.
  ISBN 1-4027-1716-4
  1. Wit and humor, Juvenile. I. Rissinger, Matt. II. Yates, Philip.
  PN6166.L58 2004
  818'.60208--dc22

               2004019280

Lot#: 10 9 8 7
08/14

Published by Sterling Publishing Co., Inc.
387 Park Avenue South, New York, NY 10016
© 2004 by Matt Rissinger and Philip Yates. Material in this book previously
appeared in *Best School Jokes Ever* © 1998, *Biggest Joke Book in the World*
© 1996, *Great Book of Zany Jokes* © 1994, *Greatest Giggles Ever* © 2002,
Greatest Jokes on Earth © 1999, *Greatest Kids' Comebacks Ever* © 2003,
It's Not My Fault Because...: The Kids' Book of Excuses © 2001, *Kids' Quickest
Comebacks* © 2004, *Totally Terrific Jokes* © 2000, *World's Silliest Jokes* © 1997
Artwork © by Jeff Sinclair.
Distributed in Canada by Sterling Publishing
c/o Canadian Manda Group, 165 Dufferin Street
Toronto, Ontario, Canada M6K 3H6
Distributed in the United Kingdom by GMC Distribution Services
Castle Place, 166 High Street, Lewes, East Sussex, England BN7 1XU
Distributed in Australia by Capricorn Link (Australia) Pty. Ltd.
P.O. Box 704, Windsor, NSW 2756, Australia

Printed in China
All rights reserved

Sterling ISBN-13: 978-1-4027-4979-7
     ISBN-10: 1-4027-4979-1

For information about custom editions, special sales, premium and
corporate purchases, please contact Sterling Special Sales
Department at 800-805-5489 or specialsales@sterlingpub.com.

CONTENTS

FOOD

Stan: Why did the silly driver suddenly get a craving for potato chips?

Dan: He saw a sign on the road that said "Dip Ahead."

Why did the green vegetable debate taking the job?

The benefits were good but the celery wasn't.

One of the kids in my neighborhood is so methodical, he once tried to arrange M&M's in alphabetical order.

Customer to attendant at fast-food restaurant:
"How much for a large Coke?"
"A dollar fifty."
"How much for a refill?"
"Refills are free."
"Great, just give me a refill."

What dessert can you eat in the ocean?
Sponge cake.

First Boy: Hey, why is it taking you so long to make Kool-Aid?
Second Boy: You try getting two quarts of water in one of these tiny envelopes!

What kind of veggies do they eat at the North Pole?
Snow peas.

❖

"Waiter, these eggs are runny."

"Why do you say that?"

"Because one just ran out the door."

❖

Rudy walked into a diner and sat down at the counter for a bite. Just as he was about to dip his hand into the pretzel bowl, he heard a voice say, "Hey, nice shirt!"

Looking around, Rudy couldn't figure out where the voice was coming from. Then he heard it again. "Hey, nice tie." Quickly, Rudy turned his head again, but still no one was there.

"Hey, nice haircut!" said the voice a third time. Just then the waitress arrived to take Rudy's order.

"Excuse me," said Rudy to the waitress, "but I keep hearing this strange voice."

"Oh, pay no attention to them," said the waitress. "That's just the pretzels. They're complimentary."

What do mannequins put on their salads?
Window dressing.

The owner of a large factory decided to make a surprise visit and check up on his staff. Walking through the plant, he noticed a young man sitting lazily in the corner.

"Just how much are you being paid a week?" said the owner angrily.

"Three hundred bucks," replied the man. Taking out a wad of bills from his wallet, the owner slapped the money into the boy's hand and said, "Here's a week's pay. Now get out and don't come back."

Turning to one of the supervisors, the owner said, "How long has that lazy bum worked here, anyway?"

"He doesn't work here," said the supervisor. "He just came to deliver a pizza."

What did the frog say when he saw a fly in his soup?

"Is that all I get?"

Hetty: What do safecrackers order when they eat out?
Betty: The combination plate.

Ziggy: What happened to the mad chef who tried to make pancakes in a volcano?
Iggy: He blew his stack.

14

Mina: Have you tried the new Hollywood citrus soda with half the calories of regular soda?
Tina: What's it called?
Mina: Lime-lite.

❖

What did the cavemen eat for lunch?
  Club sandwiches.

❖

Mr. Neutron went into a diner and ordered a soda. When he finished drinking it, he asked the waitress, "How much do I owe you?"

"For you, Mr. Neutron," she answered, "there is no charge."

❖

What's the difference between the sun and a loaf of bread?
  One rises from the East and the other from the yeast!

Little Jimmy came home from a birthday party, waving his door prize excitedly at his mother.

"Look what I won, Mom!"

"Why, it's a Thermos," said Jimmy's mother.

"What's a Thermos?" said Jimmy.

"A Thermos keeps hot things hot and cold things cold."

The next morning Jimmy packed his lunch and was about to leave for school when his mother stopped him. "Jimmy, what did you pack for lunch?

"Don't worry, mom, I have it all in my Thermos."

"What did you put in there?"

"A cup of soup and a Popsicle."

❖

Customer: I'm so hungry I could eat a horse.
Waitress: Have you heard about today's special?

Lou: My grandmother is on a new carrot diet.
Sue: Has she lost weight?
Lou: No, but she can see the scale much better.

Did you hear about the mad chef who put dynamite in his refrigerator?

It blew his cool!

Little Sara watched as her mother stuck a meat thermometer inside the turkey.

"You're not going to get me to eat that!" she said, making a sour face.

"Why not?" asked her mother.

"Because if it's that sick," said Sara, "I don't want any."

Two bananas sat on the beach sunning themselves. After a while one banana got up and left. Why?

She was starting to peel.

Clara: How did you pass the entrance exam to get into candy-making school?

Sara: It was easy. I fudged it.

"Waiter, my alphabet soup is missing a letter."
  "Oh, that must be the split P."

Arnie: What's a hot dog's favorite car?
Marnie: A Rolls.

What's a scarecrow's favorite fruit?
Strawberries.

How do corn kernels propose marriage?
They pop the question.

Sunny: My brother doesn't know how to cook.
Bunny: How can you tell?
Sunny: Because last night he burned the salad!

What do you call Egg Foo Young after it's been sitting in the refrigerator for a month?
Egg Foo Old.

What's Humpty Dumpty's least favorite meal?
Egg drop soup.

Customer: Waiter, two letters in my alphabet soup are making music.
Waiter: Oh, that must be the CDs.

Silly Sam had never cooked a day in his life but decided to surprise his wife on her birthday. He went to the barn, selected a chicken, plucked it, then popped it into the oven.

An hour later he realized he hadn't turned the oven on. When Sam pulled open the door, the chicken sat up and said, "Look, mister, either turn on the heat or give me back my feathers!"

What did the pancake say to the syrup?

"Stick with me—you'll go places."

❖

Two absentminded professors were watching TV one night. "How about a dish of ice cream?" said the first professor.

"Sounds good," replied the second professor. "I'll write it down so you won't forget."

"Don't worry, I won't forget," replied the first professor.

"But I want chocolate syrup and nuts on it."

"How could I forget that?"

A few minutes later the first professor returned with a plate of bacon and eggs.

"See, I knew I should have written it down," said the second professor. "You forgot the buttered toast!"

Lana: What cool-sounding food makes your tongue hot?
Dana: Chili.

Why didn't King Arthur like to eat at the Round Table?

He could never get a square meal there.

Customer to hostess at a bed-and-breakfast:
"Why does your dog growl at me while I'm eating? Does he want me to feed him?"
"No," said the hostess, "he's just angry because you're eating off his favorite plate."

Cindy: What do warlocks eat for breakfast?
Mindy: Deviled eggs.

"I can't figure out this jigsaw puzzle!" said the absentminded professor to his wife.

"What kind of puzzle is it?" asked the wife.

"Well, there's a rooster on the box and it has a thousand pieces inside. It's so confusing, I don't know where to start."

"It's all right, dear," said the professor's wife reassuringly. "Just put the cornflakes back in the box and go to bed."

Phil and Will went into a diner, took out their lunch boxes, and started eating their sandwiches.

"Hey!" said the waitress, "you can't eat your own sandwiches in here."

So Phil and Will swapped sandwiches.

What did the saltcellar say to the pepper mill?
"Let's shake on it!"

At an all-you-can-eat restaurant Joey came back to the table, his plate full for the fifth time.

"Joey!" exclaimed his mother. "Doesn't it embarrass you that people have seen you go up to the buffet table five times?"

"Not a bit," said Joey, "I just tell them I'm filling up the plate for you!"

A hungry man saw a sign in a restaurant window saying, "We'll pay $100 to anyone who orders something we can't make."

When he was seated at his table he said to the waitress, "I'll have an elephant sandwich." Digging into her apron, the waitress pulled out a roll of bills and handed the man a hundred dollars.

"What?" said the man as he pocketed the
money, "no elephants today?"

"Oh, we have elephants, all right," sighed
the waitress. "But we're all out of the big rolls."

How Do They Like Their Eggs?

Sunbathers like their eggs fried.

Cable-TV repairmen like their eggs scrambled.

Meteorologists like their eggs sunny-side up.

Robin Hood likes his eggs poached.

Detectives like their eggs hard-boiled.

Absentminded professors like their eggs cracked.

Kids taking tests like their eggs over easy.

What's the official hot dog of the Academy Awards?

Oscar Mayer wieners.

Mack: What do you call a turkey the day after Thanksgiving?
Jack: Leftovers.

Wes: How do you make a cream puff?
Les: Chase it around the block a few times.

What happens when lettuce is arrested for a crime?

It's innocent until proven wilty.

Gene: Why did the waiter serve the physician a peanut butter and cucumber sandwich?
Irene: Because that's just what the doctor ordered.

ANIMALS

Where do cows, pigs, sheep, ducks, and horses go to get their prescriptions filled?

Old MacDonald's Farm-acy.

A frog expert from the aquarium visited a third-grade class to give a talk on amphibians.

"It's easy to tell the male frogs from the female frogs," said the man, as he held up two cages. "When you feed them, the male frog will eat only female flies, and the female frogs will eat only male flies."

One boy in the back of the room raised his hand. "But how do you tell which flies are male and which are female?" he asked.

"How should I know?" replied the man. "I'm a frog expert."

❖

Hank: This morning I woke up and felt the dog licking my face.
Frank: What's so bad about that?
Hank: We don't have a dog.

Two hens were pecking around the yard when suddenly a softball came sailing over the fence, landing a few feet away from them.

Said the first hen to the second, "Gosh, will you just look at the ones they're turning out next door?"

How do you turn a beagle into a bird?
Remove the "b."

How do Boy Scout whales start fires?
They rub two fish sticks together.

Dennis and his friends were boasting about
their cats.

"I taught my cat to fetch my slippers," said Hank.

"That's nothing. I taught my cat to get the
newspaper in the morning," said Ralphie.

"You think that's so good?" bragged Dennis.
"Just wait'll you see the video of my dog burying
a bone."

"What does your dog have to do with it?"
asked Hank.

"My cat," said Dennis, "was operating the
video camera."

Teacher: Do you think Noah did a lot of fishing on the ark?

Class Clown: What, with only two worms?

What did the worm say when it ate its way into the cucumber?

"I'm really in a pickle now!"

Clint: What happened to the turtle that stepped on an electric wire?

Flint: He was shell-shocked.

Judy: I finally trained my dog not to beg at the table.

Trudy: How did you do that?

Judy: I let him taste my sister's cooking.

Five insects rented rooms on the top floor of an apartment building while five rented rooms on the lower floor. What are these insects called?

Ten-ants.

How do you turn a sparrow into a weapon?

Remove the "s" and the "p."

What do bees brush their hair with?

Honeycombs.

What happened to the zebra that was court-martialed?
It lost its stripes.

Teddie: My dog is a carpenter.
Eddie: What makes you say that?
Teddie: Last night he made a bolt for the door.

One day Mrs. Hennessey looked out at her driveway and saw her postman exchanging papers with a suspicious-looking man in dark glasses. When the man strode off, she confronted the postal worker with what she had seen. He then confessed that he was actually a spy for the CIA.

"You sure took a chance," said Mrs. Hennessey. "My dog is trained to attack strangers."

"There's no need to worry about that," the mailman reassured her. "He's one of us."

Did you hear about the turtle that was mugged by a snail? When the police asked for a description of the suspect, the turtle replied, "I don't know. It all happened so fast . . ."

Mickey: Why are fish such terrible tennis players?
Ricky: They're afraid to get too close to the net.

Two buffalo were grazing contentedly on the open prairie when a cowboy rode up. Looking the animals over, he shook his head and said, "You two are the ugliest buffalo I ever saw. Look at you—your fur is tangled, you have humps on your backs, and you slobber all over the place."

As the cowboy rode off, the first buffalo remarked to the second, "I think I just heard a discouraging word."

Did you hear about the eel that got lost at the mall?
It went on a shocking spree.

A woman walked into a pet shop and told the owner she needed two large rats and a dozen cockroaches.

"What do you need them for?"

"Because," said the woman, "I'm moving and my lease says that when I move I must leave the apartment in the same condition as I found it."

What would you get if you crossed a dragon and the best man at a wedding?

A guy who really knows how to toast the bride and groom.

A panda walked into a restaurant and ordered a bamboo salad. When the panda had finished eating, he suddenly pulled out a gun and fired it into the ceiling. After a moment, the panda got up, paid his bill, and started for the door.

"Wait just a minute!" said the waitress angrily, "why did you do that?"

"Because I read it in an encyclopedia," said the panda.

"Encyclopedia?" said the waitress, "what does it say in the encyclopedia?"

"Look it up," said the panda. "It says, 'The panda eats bamboo shoots and leaves.'"

Stu: What side of a killer shark should you stay away from?
Lou: The inside.

What kind of CDs do fish listen to?
Sole music.

What animal always takes a bath with its shoes on?
A horse!

A woman frantically dialed 911. "You've got to help me," she said. "I've lost my dog!"

"Sorry, miss," said the dispatcher, "but we don't handle missing animals."

"But you don't understand. This is no ordinary dog. He can talk."

"Well, you better hang up, he might be trying to call in."

Tex: What has 12 tails and 1 horn and squeals?
Lex: A dozen pigs in a pickup truck.

Jason: I finally found the rattle in my car.
Mason: I'm glad to hear it.
Jason: I'm not—it was attached to a snake!

What is the favorite food of the Three Musketeers?
Swordfish.

Floyd: What do you get when you cross a cat with
a porcupine?
Lloyd: An animal that goes "meowch" whenever it
licks itself.

Farmer Dill: Does your cow have bells around
its neck?
Farmer Will: Why should it have bells when it's
already got two horns?

What would you get if you crossed a chicken with a genie?

A rooster that grants you three wishbones.

City Slicker: Well, I finally went for a ride this morning.
Dude Ranch Hand: Horseback?
City Slicker: Yep, he got back about an hour before I did.

"Look, Mom!" said Billy when he and his mother arrived at the country store. Posted on the glass door was a sign saying, "Danger! Beware of Dog!" Carefully, Billy and his mom entered the store, only to find a harmless old hound dog asleep on the floor.

"Is that the dog we're supposed to be afraid of?" said Billy to the storekeeper.

"That's him," replied the man.

"But the sign makes it sound like he's dangerous," said Billy.

"He is," said the storekeeper. "Before I posted that sign, people kept tripping over him."

What's the difference between a person who has hope and an insect that leaves the hive?

One's a believer, the other's a bee leaver.

What's the difference between a child's toy and a newborn snake?

One's a baby rattler, the other's a rattler's baby.

A frog went to visit a fortune-teller. "What do you see in my future?" asked the frog.

"Very soon," replied the fortune-teller, "you will meet a pretty young girl who will want to know everything about you."

"That's great!" said the frog, hopping up and down excitedly. "But when will I meet her?"

"Next week in science class," said the fortune-teller.

What do you call a fish with no eyes?

Fsh!

Chickie: What do you get if you cross an elephant and a rooster?
Dickie: An animal that never forgets to wake you up in the morning.

What is the definition of a slug?

A snail with a housing problem!

What kind of suit would you wear to a kangaroo wedding?

A jumpsuit.

A man brought a rabbit, a frog, and a chicken to a talent agent's office. As the agent watched with disinterest, the frog drank from a glass of water while the rabbit danced around the chicken and performed somersaults.

Just as the agent was about to toss the man and his animals out the door, the rabbit took a bow and said, "Thank you and good night!"

"That's incredible!" said the agent. "The hare is hired."

"But what about the frog?" said the man.

"The frog has no talent, I want the rabbit," replied the agent.

"But the chicken—" said the man.

"No chicken, I want the rabbit!" the agent insisted. The next week the agent got the rabbit a spot on a TV variety show. When it was introduced, the rabbit hopped onstage, cleared its throat, and then quietly walked off.
"What happened?" said the agent to the owner.

"The rabbit didn't talk!"

"Talk?" said the owner. "The rabbit doesn't talk."

"But last week I heard it—"

"I tried to tell you."

"Tell me what?"

"About the chicken. He's a ventriloquist."

Moe: How is a Doberman in the desert like a frankfurter?

Joe: I don't know.

Moe: They're both hot dogs.

Why don't people like to take checks from kangaroos?
Because they might bounce.

What did one mule say to the other?

"I get a kick out of you."

A man went to the zoo for the first time and watched as the zookeeper fed a hungry four-legged animal.

"Gosh, I wonder what that wolf would say if he could talk," the man said to the zookeeper.

"He'd probably say, "I'm a hyena, dummy,' " replied the zookeeper.

What romantic song do fish sing?

"Salmon-chanted Evening!"

Why did the mosquito go to the dentist?

To improve his bite!

Why do kangaroos love Club Med?

They hate paying out-of-pocket expenses.

What do you call a cat with a pager?
  A beeping tom.

Willie: How am I going to write an essay on an elephant?
Tillie: First, you're going to need a big ladder.

A professor who collected birds went into an exotic pet shop and said, "I want a parrot that talks."

"I have just the parrot for you," said the owner, and he led the man to a cage where a very distinguished-looking parrot stood on a perch.

"Speak, Philmore!" said the pet shop owner.

Without missing a beat, Philmore spoke in a classically trained voice. "Where there's a will, there's a way. Crime doesn't pay. Money is the root of all evil."

"Pretty good, huh?" said the shopkeeper.

"How much?" said the professor.

"Three thousand dollars."

"Forget it," the professor said as he made his way to the door. "For that kind of money, I want a parrot that writes his own stuff."

A woman in a butcher shop spotted a dog waiting at the counter.

"How much ground beef do you need today?" said the butcher to the dog. The dog barked twice and with that, the butcher wrapped up two pounds of ground beef.

"How many pork chops today?" said the butcher. The dog barked four times and the butcher wrapped up four pork chops.

Grabbing the packages in his mouth, the dog headed out the door and trotted down the street. Curious, the woman followed the dog to an apartment house and watched as the animal pressed the doorbell with his nose.

When an old man opened the door, the woman remarked to the owner, "You sure have a smart dog there."

"Smart? Are you kidding?" said the old man. "This is the third time this week he forgot his key."

Chuckie: What's worse than looking into the eye of a great white shark?

Duckie: Looking into his tonsils.

❖

Why did the snake swallow the flashlight?

It wanted to shed some light.

What has 100 feet and 98 shoes?

A centipede trying on a new pair of sneakers.

First Octopus: What do you hate most about being an octopus?

Second Octopus: Washing my hands before dinner.

What did one termite say to the other?
"Want to share a house with me?"

What do you call the winner of a barnyard beauty contest?
The Dairy Queen.

Flip: I just bought a talking parrot for a thousand dollars.

Skip: What does it say?

Flip: "You paid too much, you paid too much!"

What is a woodpecker's favorite kind of joke?
A knock-knock.

Mack: What would you get if you crossed a dog and a lamb?

Jack: A sheep that can round itself up!

Why did the snowman call his dog Frost?
Because Frost bites.

What did the dog say to the flea?
  "I'll be your host this evening."

Flo: Why do you never see zebras in the army?
Joe: Because they've already earned their stripes.

Why was the young whale sent to the principal?
  For spouting off at the teacher.

Rudy: Why did the lamb like the buffet restaurant?
Judy: Because the menu said "All Ewe Can Eat."

Henry jumped for joy when his parents bought him two rabbits for his birthday. Although he played with them every day, the little bunnies soon proved a nuisance to Henry's parents. When not in their cage, they gnawed on the furniture and left rabbit droppings all over the house.

When one of the rabbits chewed up his slipper, Henry's father lost his temper.

"If that happens again," he shouted, "we're going to have one of those rabbits for dinner!"

"Gee, that's great," said Henry, his face lighting up. "Do you think I can teach him how to hold a spoon?"

What did the shrimp do with the big diamond ring?
He prawned it!

Dilly: I crossed a cat with a stove and guess
what I got?
Willy: A self-cleaning oven.

Customer: May I have a pair of alligator shoes?
Salesman: Certainly. What size is your alligator?

❖

How does a paramecium call home?
On a single-cell phone.

❖

What would you get if you crossed a parrot
with a pig?
A squawky bird that hogs the conversation.

❖

What's black-and-white, furry, and doesn't ever
want to grow up?
Peter Panda.

❖

Did you hear about the cats that moved next
door to the mice? They wanted to have the
neighbors over for dinner.

Why don't elephants like their kids to walk in line?

They believe children should be seen, not herded.

What did the boy do when his pet rodent used bad words?

He washed his mouse out with soap.

Joe: What do you get if you cross a chicken and a parrot?

Moe: A bird that lays an egg and talks about it.

Gomer: What do steering wheels and stool pigeons have in common?

Homer: Sooner or later, they both turn on you.

My dog is so lazy, he hires other dogs to chase cats for him.

Mindy: Why was the cockatoo first in line at the beauty parlor?

Cindy: Because the early bird gets the perm.

What dogs work for the telephone company?
Labrador receivers.

Mandy: I'm reading about a turtle that falls in love with a toupee.
Sandy: What's it called?
Mandy: The Tortoise and the Hare.

GHOULISH

Homer: Why did the vampire flunk out of art class?
Gomer: Because he could only draw blood.

Homer: Did you hear about the monster with five legs?
Gomer: No, but I bet his pants fit him like a glove.

Why did the witch come to school dressed as a spoon?
She wanted to stir things up.

A radioactive monster burst into a clothing store. "I can't keep my pants up," cried the monster. "Do you have any suspenders?"

"Sorry," replied the clerk. "But might I suggest ja belt for your toxic waist?"

What was the Invisible Man raised on?
Evaporated milk.

What is gruesome, flies, and goes "Cough-cough"?
A witch in a dust storm!

Why is it hard to celebrate Father's Day in Egypt?
The are more mummies than daddies

What do wizards say when they cast the wrong spell?
Hex-cuse me.

Dilly: Do vampires act in movies?
Silly: Yes, they get bit parts.

Monster: I've changed my mind.
Dr. Frankenstein: Good, does the new one work
any better?

Gene: What do you get when you cross a dragon on Valentine's Day?
Irene: Heartburn.

Who is the best dancer at a monster party?
The Boogeyman.

Lem and Clem were close friends and bowling buddies for many years. One day they made a vow that whoever died first would send a message back to the other.

A week later Clem died, and for many days Lem missed his bowling buddy. One night Clem's ghost appeared in Lem's bedroom.

"Tell me, Clem," said Lem excitedly, "is there bowling in heaven?"

"I have good news and bad news," replied Clem's ghost. "The good news is that there's bowling every day."

"What's the bad news?" asked Lem.

"The bad news," said Clem, "is that starting tomorrow you're captain of the team."

What classic TV comedy deals with ghosts
stranded on an island?
Ghoul-igan's Island.

Where did the monster keep her extra fingers?
In her handbag.

What happened when the tree saw the ghost?
It was petrified.

What did the skeleton order at the restaurant?
Spare ribs.

What would you get if you crossed an author
and a vampire?
A book you can really sink your teeth into.

Why didn't the skeleton go to the ball?
Because he had no body to go with.

Franny: Why did Godzilla hang out at the
computer store on Halloween?
Danny: So he could bob for Apples.

What do monsters play on rainy days?
Musical scares.

What did the mummy say when the archeologist
discovered his tomb?
For a while there, I thought I was a lost gauze.

Vance: What do you get when you give Frankenstein a rabbit's brain?
Lance: A monster with a lot of harebrained ideas.

What did Dracula's mother hang over his crib?
A blood mobile.

Why was the Invisible Man heartbroken?

Because his girlfriend told him she couldn't see him anymore.

What would you get if you crossed a ghost with a pair of trousers?

Scaredy-pants.

Baby Dragon: Mommy, Mommy I had a terrible dream where a guy in a tin suit was chasing me with a sword!

Mommy Dragon: There, there, dear—that was just a knight-mare.

Why didn't the Abominable Snowman get married?

He got cold feet.

What do dragons call brave knights?

Toast.

Snip: What do you get if you cross nursery rhymes with scary stories?

Snap: Mother Goose Bumps.

Why did the Invisible Man's son flunk third grade?

His teacher kept marking him absent.

Why don't witches ride their brooms when they're angry?

They might fly off the handle.

Ghoul Zed: Who shall I invite to our Halloween party?

Ghoul Ted: Anyone you can dig up.

Did you hear about the vampire who was a failure?

He fainted at the sight of blood.

Dill: Was Dracula ever married?
Will: No, he's always been a bat-chelor.

Was the vampire race close?
 Yes, it was neck and neck.

75

In what kind of restaurant would you never find a vampire?

A stake house.

How many witches does it take to change a lightbulb?

Just one, but she changes it into a toad.

Lem: What do you get when you cross Godzilla with the Invisible Man?
Clem: A great big nothing!

Sign at a funeral home:

Drive Carefully,
We'll Wait.

What would you get if you crossed a witch with a gourmet chef?

An eight-curse meal.

What would you get if you crossed a vampire and a snowman?

Frostbite.

Why don't skeletons play music in a church?

Because they have no organs!

SCHOOL JOKES

What did the pencil say to the piece of paper?
"I dot my i's on you."

How did the trombone manage to pass first grade?
The teacher let it slide.

The human brain is a wonderful thing. It starts working the moment you get up in the morning and doesn't stop until the teacher calls on you.

❖

The meanest principal in the world was worried that his private school would close because of a lack of students. One day he called in his overworked assistant and demanded that he go out and recruit more students or be fired.

The next day five new students signed up. The day after that another ten signed up. Within a week the enrollment was sky-high. Pulling his assistant aside one day, the principal asked, "How did you get so many new students to sign up?"

"It was easy," replied the assistant. "I just started a rumor that you were quitting."

Jack: Hey, Mom, I learned five new letters today!
Mom: Oh, yes? Which ones?
Jack: F-L-U-N-K.

Dad: If you passed your exam, why did the teacher fail you?
Chad: Because I passed it to the kid next to me.

When Mrs. Spencer, the third-grade teacher, gave a big test to her students, Harold, the son of a millionaire, knew there was no way he could pass. Reaching into his pocket, he found a $100 bill and attached it to the test with a note saying, "A dollar per point." The next day when Harold got his test back there was a note saying, "Good try!" along with $60 in change.

Dad: I'm sorry you flunked your math test. How far were you from the right answer?
Tad: Three seats!

Art teacher to student:
"What is that a picture of?"
"That's me when I accidentally hammered my finger."
"Oh, it's a self-portrait?"
"No, just a thumbnail sketch."

"What did you think of the magician at the assembly?" the teacher asked Philip.

"He wasn't very good," replied Philip. "But the teacher he sawed in half was terrific!"

Teacher: How did Webster invent the dictionary?
Helen: He got into an argument and one word led to another.

Principal: Isn't this your second warning not to misbehave in history class?

Class Clown: Yes, but, as you know, history repeats itself.

Teacher: Do you think you can sleep in my class?

Pupil: Well, I could if you didn't talk so loud.

Mom: How did you manage to flunk history?

Nicky: Because everything the teacher says goes in both ears and out the other.

Mom: But that's three ears!

Nicky: I'm not doing well in math, either.

To encourage all his students to become smarter, the principal at a grade school hung a sign above the bathroom sink with one word on it: "THINK!"

The next day somebody hung another sign above the soap dispenser saying: "THOAP!"

When school finally let out for summer vacation, one teacher said to another, "Boy, you should have heard the excitement. When the bell rang, everyone stomped their feet and shouted for joy!"

"It was pretty wild, huh?" remarked the second teacher.

"You bet it was!" replied the first. "And that was just in the teachers' lounge!"

❖

Principal: Why did you run into Mrs. Leary's math class when I was chasing you?
Class Clown: I was told there's safety in numbers.

When the teacher gave the class a true/false test, Frank was ready for it. Reaching into his pocket, he dug out a coin and flipped it for each question. Heads for true, tails for false.

Later, when the rest of the class had gone off to lunch, Frank was still flipping the coin. "What's taking you so long to finish?" asked his teacher.

"Oh, I finished a long time ago," said Frank. "Now I'm just checking my answers."

Principal: Why were you acting up at orchestra practice?
Class Clown: I guess I just don't know how to conduct myself.

One morning Lenny and Benny were late for their mathematics exam. Thinking quickly, the boys rubbed some grease on their face and hands, and decided on a good excuse. By the time they got to the classroom, the other students had already finished and left. "Sorry, Mrs. Quinn," said Lenny, "but I was giving

Benny a ride on my bike and we got a flat tire and had to stop and get it fixed."

"Come back on Monday," said Mrs. Quinn, "and I'll let you take the test."

A few days later they came back for the makeup test. Mrs. Quinn put each boy into a separate room with their test questions. The first question was easy and worth 5 points. The second question was worth 95 points. It read simply, "Which tire?"

❖

Dad: Did you pass algebra?
Tom: I sure did.
Dad: Then what is this "F" on your report card?
Tom: Because every time I came to school I passed right by algebra class.

The art teacher instructed her students to do a self-portrait. When Willy handed his in, the teacher took one look at it and said, "But, Willy, this isn't you."

"That's right," replied Willy. "It's a self-portrait of someone else."

Teacher: Why did you copy Larry's test?
Seymour: What gave me away?
Teacher: His name on your paper.

What happened to the composer who failed all his subjects?

He was held Bach a year.

One day the school troublemaker was sent to the principal's office.

"Do you know why you're here?" asked the principal.

"Is it about this morning?" asked the troublemaker.

"Your teacher says you ran in the hall, beat up two students, started a food fight in the cafeteria, and cursed at one of your classmates."

"Boy, that's a relief," sighed the troublemaker. "I thought maybe you found out I broke your windshield."

A little boy knocked on the door of the teachers' lounge and said, "Did anyone lose $50 attached to a rubber band?"

"Why, yes," said one of the teachers.

"Well, today's your lucky day," said the boy. "I found the rubber band."

Manny: I finally made it out of the third grade.
Danny: What happened?
Manny: We had a fire drill.

Why did the giraffe graduate early?
She was head and shoulders above the rest.

How many substitute teachers does it take to change a lightbulb?
None—they just leave it dark and show a movie.

What do cats read in the morning?
U.S. Mews and World Report.

Mr. Harper, the English teacher, asked Mary to give him a sentence with an object.

"You are very handsome," replied Mary.

"Good," said Mr. Harper, "but what is the object?"

"To get an A in English," said Mary.

Why was the pony sent to the principal's office?
For horsing around.

Juan: Do smart chickens go to school?
Don: Of course, how else do you think we get Grade A eggs?

Where do frogs keep notes?
On lily pads.

"All right, everybody on their backs with their feet up in the air!" the gym teacher shouted to his third-grade class. "I want you to pretend you're riding a bicycle."

Dropping to the floor, the students began rapidly kicking their legs in the air—all except for one boy who slowly moved one leg in the air while keeping the other on the floor.

"What's wrong?" asked the gym teacher.

"Isn't it obvious?" said the boy. "I've got a flat."

❖

Art Teacher: What did you draw?
Mason: A cop chasing a robber.
Art Teacher: But I don't see any robber.
Mason: That's because he got away.

Teacher: Lenny, did you write this absentee note that was supposed to be from your parents?

Lenny: What gave you that idea?

Teacher: Because it says, "Dear Teacher, Please excuse Lenny for being sick March 30, 31, 32, and 33."

Mother: How was your first day at school?

Tommy: Okay, but the teacher didn't give me a present.

Mother: Why would she give you a present?

Tommy: Because she said, "Tom, sit there for the present."

Joe: My teacher says she's sick and tired of my appearance.

Bo: What's wrong with your appearance?

Joe: I haven't made one since school started.

Notice on bulletin board:

> *There will be a meeting of*
> *the Mind Readers Club at . . .*
> *well, you know what time.*

Music Teacher: Cindy, would you take a note to your mother?
Cindy: Sure, how about a B flat?

"Son, the reason you're getting bad grades is that you spend too much time watching game shows."

"I'm sorry, Dad, but you'll have to phrase that in the form of a question."

What do math teachers take for a cold?
Alka-Seltzer Plus.

What would you get if you crossed a librarian with a race-car driver?

A speed reader.

Mom: Why were you expelled from school?
Tom: I used a hose to fill up the swimming pool.
Mom: But your school doesn't have a pool.
Tom: It does now.

Hank: I think we're going to get a pop quiz tomorrow on the digestive system.
Tank: What makes you say that?
Hank: I have a gut feeling.

Mom: This is the worst report card ever. What do you have to say for yourself?
Tom: Look on the bright side—at least I'm not cheating.

What do dragons like most about school?
The fire drills.

What kind of tests are fish good at?
Open-brook tests.

Woody got up in front of the class and read his book report aloud. When he finished, the teacher said, "That was very good, and I'm so glad you didn't tell us what happens at the end."

"Well," said Woody proudly, "I figured if they wanted to know the ending, they could do what I did and rent the video."

Father: Son, what kind of marks do you expect to get in gym class?
Son: No marks, Dad, just a lot of bruises.

While on a field trip to an amusement park, the teacher lost his wallet. Gathering the group together, he told the kids, "My wallet had $300 in it. I will give a $20 reward to anyone who finds it."

A voice from the back of the group chimed in, "And I'll give $25!"

How can you tell when the school cook uses too much pepper?

Her specialty is toasted sneeze sandwiches.

One of the kids in my English class is so dumb he thinks a prefix is what you do before you break something.

Joey Smith got so good at forging signatures, he began charging his friends to write absentee notes for them. One day the principal found out and called him into the office.

"Well, Joey," said the principal, "you'd better have a good excuse for me."

"I do," Joey replied. "But it'll cost you."

Excuses, Excuses

From a nutty professor: "On Friday my son will be absentminded."

From the Invisible Man: "If you don't see my daughter in school this week, it doesn't mean she isn't there."

From a time-machine inventor: "My son will not be in school on Friday, but he will show up the previous Tuesday."

From an orchestra conductor: "Please excuse my son as he thinks he's a xylophone. Until he improves, would you please play along with him?"

KNOCK-KNOCKS

Knock-knock.
  Who's there?
Apollo G.
  Apollo G. who?
Apollo G. accepted.

Knock-knock.

Who's there?

Butternut.

Butternut who?

Butternut talk back to the teacher.

Knock-knock.
Who's there?
Camphor.
Camphor who?
Camphor get my homework again.

Knock-knock.
Who's there?
Canal.
Canal who?
Canal come out and play with me?

Knock-knock.
Who's there?
Children's Day.
Children's Day who?
Children's Day the darndest things!

Knock-knock.
 Who's there?
CIA.
 CIA who?
C, I Ate the whole cake!

Knock-knock.
 Who's there?
Closure.
 Closure who?
Closure mouth when you eat!

Knock-knock.
 Who's there?
Comma.
 Comma who?
Comma little closer and give me a kiss!

Knock-knock.
Who's there?
Diploma.
Diploma who?
Diploma's here to fix di bathtub.

Knock-knock.
Who's there?
Dishes.
Dishes who?
Dishes mission control speaking.

Knock-knock.
Who's there?
Donut.
Donut who?
Donut make me wait here another minute.

Knock-knock.
  Who's there?
Dozen.
  Dozen who?
Dozen look like rain.

Jack: Knock-knock.
Jill: Who's there?
Jack: Eiffel.
Jill: Eiffel who?
Jack: Eiffel down and broke my crown.

Knock-knock.
  Who's there?
Emerson.
  Emerson who?
Emerson ugly shoes!

Knock-knock.
  Who's there?
Evan.
  Evan who?
Evan knows what they put in the cafeteria food.

Knock-knock.
  Who's there?
Felon.
  Felon who?
Felon my head and got
three stitches!

THESE JOKES REALLY **KNOCK** ME OUT!

Knock-knock.
  Who's there?
Four E's.
  Four E's who?
Four E's a jolly good fellow . . . !

Knock-knock.
  Who's there?
Freighter.
  Freighter who?
Freighter ghosts, aren't you?

Knock-knock.
  Who's there?
Gruesome.
  Gruesome who?
Gruesome since the last time I saw you.

Knock-knock.
Who's there?
Harmony.
Harmony who?
Harmony times I gotta
ring this bell?

Knock-knock.
Who's there?
Hiya.
Hiya who?
Hiya someone to fix the doorbell!

Knock-knock.
Who's there?
Howie.
Howie who?
Fine, thanks. How're you?

Knock-knock.
Who's there?
Hygiene.
Hygiene who?
Hygiene, how ya' doin'?

Knock-knock.
Who's there?
Imus.
Imus who?
Imus get an A on my math test.

Knock-knock.
Who's there?
Isthmus.
Isthmus who?
Isthmus be love. Kiss me!

Knock-knock.
Who's there?
Ivan
Ivan Who?
"Ivan working on the railroad, all
the live long day!"

Knock-knock.
Who's there?
Ivan
Ivan Who?
"Ivan to hold your hand.

Knock-knock.
Who's there?
Juicy.
Juicy who?
Juicy that shooting star?

Knock-knock.
  Who's there?
Kenya.
  Kenya who?
Kenya lend me five dollars, I'm broke!

Knock-knock.
  Who's there?
Liver.
  Liver who?
Liver 'round here?

Knock-knock.
  Who's there?
Marmoset.
  Marmoset who?
Marmoset the car keys down and lost 'em again.

Knock-knock.
Who's there?
Lettuce.
Lettuce who?
Lettuce be a lesson to you!

Knock-knock.
Who's there?
Noah.
Noah who?
Noah 'bout how to build an ark?

Knock-knock.
Who's there?
Nova.
Nova who?
Nova good place to eat around here?

Knock-knock.
Who's there?
Omelet.
Omelet who?
Omelet smarter than I look.

Knock-knock.
Who's there?
Osborn.
Osborn who?
Osborn in a hospital, where were you born?

Knock-knock.
Who's there?
Pasture.
Pasture who?
Pasture bedtime, isn't it?

Knock-knock.
Who's there?
Pecan.
Pecan who?
Pecan the cookie jar and see if there's any left.

Knock-knock.
Who's there?
Phyllis.
Phyllis who?
Phyllis pitcher up with lemonade.

Knock-knock.
Who's there?
Pooch and Jimmy.
Pooch and Jimmy who?
Pooch your arms around me and Jimmy a kiss.

Knock-knock.
Who's there?
Pudding.
Pudding who?
Pudding your pants on before your underwear is
a bad idea.

Knock-knock.
Who's there?
Roach.
Roach who?
Roach you a letter, but you never wrote back.

Knock-knock.

Who's there?

Sanctuary.

Sanctuary who?

Sanctuary much for answering the door.

Knock-knock.

Who's there?

Senior.

Senior who?

Senior through the window so I know you're there!

Knock-knock.

Who's there?

Shirley.

Shirley who?

Shirley you could open the door for me.

Knock-knock.
Who's there?
Spillane.
Spillane who?
Spillane to me what's going on.

Knock-knock.
Who's there?
Summons.
Summons who?
Summons at the door.

Knock-knock.
Who's there?
Sun bear.
Sun bear who?
"Sun bear over the rainbow . . ."

Knock-knock.
Who's there?
Sushi.
Sushi who?
Sushi says to me, "Let's dance!"

Knock-knock.
Who's there?
Thesis.
Thesis who?
Thesis a stickup!

Knock-knock.
Who's there?
Thor.
Thor who?
Thor loser, aren't you?

Knock-knock.
Who's there?
Toulouse.
Toulouse who?
Toulouse ten pounds, I have to exercise every day.

Knock-knock.
Who's there?
Unaware.
Unaware who?
Unaware is what you put on before your pants.

Knock-knock.
Who's there?
Weirdo.
Weirdo who?
Weirdo the deer and antelope play?

DOCTOR, DOCTOR

While Hubert waited to see his doctor, he heard a shout from behind the wall, "Measles! Typhoid! Tetanus!"

"Doctor, is the nurse all right?" said Hubert to his doctor.

"Oh, don't worry about her," replied the doctor. "She just likes to call the shots around here."

Floyd: Doctor, everyone thinks I'm a liar.
Doctor: I find that hard to believe.

Three absentminded professors went to the doctor for a memory test. The doctor asked the first professor, "What's three times three?"

The first professor said, "278."

"What's three times three?" the doctor asked the second professor.

"Saturday," replied the second professor.

"What's three times three?" the doctor asked the third professor.

"Three times three is nine," said the third professor.

"That's great!" said the doctor. "How did you figure it out?"

"It was easy," replied the professor. "I simply subtracted 278 from Saturday."

Doctor: Did those pills I gave you improve your memory?
Patient: Yes, but who are you?

Patient: Last night I dreamed I was trapped inside a washing machine.
Doctor: What did you do?
Patient: What could I do? I tossed and turned all night.

❖

Charlie's doctor was a real quack. One day Charlie went for a checkup and his doctor said, "Please strip to the waist."

When Charlie had removed his shirt, the doctor said, "When I hit you on the back, cough."

The doctor hit him on the back and Charlie coughed. For the next several seconds he kept hitting Charlie, and Charlie kept coughing.

Finally, the doctor shook his head and said, "How long have you had this cough, anyway?"

How did the Norse god take his temperature?
With a Thor-mometer.

Nurse: May I dress your cut?
Patient: Why, don't you like what it's wearing?

"Doctor, Doctor, I think I'm a trampoline!"

"Don't worry, you'll bounce back in no time."

A father was having a hard time getting his son to the dentist. He finally pulled him, yelling, into the office. The father picked up his son, put him in the chair, and sat down to read a magazine. Before he got it open, he heard a scream. Losing his temper, the father yelled, "What's going on?" An older voice cried out, "He bit my finger!"

Doctor to patient:
"I have good news and bad news. The bad news is, you have a terrible, horrible new unnamed disease."

"What's the good news?"

"The good news is, I get to name the disease after me and become horribly rich and terribly famous."

Kramer: Doctor, how do I keep from losing my hair?
Doctor: Write your name on your toupee.

Husband: My wife talks to her plants.
Doctor: What's wrong with that?
Husband: On the telephone?

Patient: Doctor, you've got to help me. Some mornings I wake up and think I'm Donald Duck; other mornings I think I'm Mickey Mouse.
Doctor: Hmmm, how long have you been having these Disney spells?

Hospitilized Patient: Hey, Doc, you've already removed my appendix, tonsils, and adenoids. Will I ever get out of this place?
Doctor: Don't worry, you're getting out—bit by bit.

Wracked with fever, Benny rang Dr. Godfrey's doorbell at three in the morning. Dragging himself out of bed, the doctor opened the door and said, "Well?"

"No," replied Benny, "sick."

"Doctor, Doctor, every night my foot falls asleep."

"What's wrong with that?"

"It snores."

Sign at microbiology lab: "Staph Only."

Woman: My mother-in-law thinks she's a parachute.
Doctor: What's wrong with that?
Woman: She keeps dropping in unannounced.

Mother: Doctor, you're a quack. My kid isn't getting any better.

Doctor: Did you give him the medicine I prescribed?

Mother: Absolutely not! The bottle said "Keep out of the reach of children."

Little Priscilla went to the school nurse and said, "My head hurts, my belly hurts, and my arms and legs hurt."

After checking the girl over, the nurse pulled out a tiny hammer and tapped Priscilla's knees to check her reflexes.

"How do you feel now?" asked the nurse.

"Worse!" groaned Priscilla. "Now my knees hurt."

School nurse to sick boy:

"What is your name, so we can notify your parents?"

"Don't worry, my parents already know my name."

The acupuncturist's assistant came into the office and watched as the doctor was about to stick a needle into an empty bed.

"Are you feeling all right, doctor?" asked the assistant.

"I'm fine," replied the acupuncturist, "but this invisible man needs help."

Dan: My doctor says I have Ferris Wheel flu.
Stan: I heard something was going around.

A boy took his limping dog to the vet and said, "I want to know if my dog is faking or if he really has an injured paw. Can you help me?"

"Certainly," replied the vet. The vet opened the door, snapped his fingers, and a beautiful Siamese cat walked in. The cat jumped up on the table where the dog lay, sniffed it up and down, then leaped off and disappeared into the other room.

"Yes, your dog's paw is really hurt," said the vet. "That'll be $200."

"Why so much money?" asked the boy.

"That's $50 for me," said the vet, "and $150 for the CAT scan."

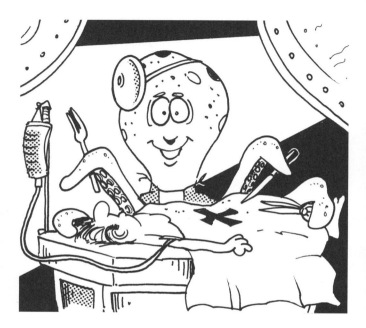

What do you call a surgeon with eight arms?
A doc-topus.

Why did Humpty Dumpty go to the psychiatrist?
He was cracking up.

❖

Danny's mother gave birth to twins. One day after
school his father took him to the hospital for a
visit. While waiting to see his mother, Danny
wandered into another room where a woman was
lying in bed with a plaster cast on her foot.

"How long have you been here?" Danny asked
the woman.

"About a week," groaned the woman.

"But where's your baby?" asked Danny.

"I don't have a baby."

"Gee, what's taking you so long?" said Danny.
"My mom's only been here a day and she's already
got two of them."

Dentist: I'll pull your aching tooth out in five minutes.

Patient: How much will it cost?

Dentist: One hundred dollars.

Patient: That much for just five minutes?

Dentist: Well, if you prefer, I can pull it out very slowly.

I CAN'T BELIEVE IT... YOU'RE GIVING ME THE BRUSH OFF ?!!

Patient to hospital administrator:

"I'm here to file a complaint."

"What's the complaint?"

"The doctor used a four-letter word during surgery."

"What word was that?"

"Oops!"

❖

A man who had lived a long and happy life was lying on his deathbed when the aroma of his wife's chocolate chip cookies filled the air.

"My time has come," said the old man when his wife stepped into the room. "But before I die, I would like to have one last nibble of your delicious chocolate chip cookies."

"I'm afraid that's out of the question," answered his wife. "Those are for the family after the funeral."

139

Stuffy: Doctor, how can I keep my chest cold from going to my head?

Doctor: Try tying a knot in your neck.

❖

"Doctor, Doctor, I think I'm suffering from déjà vu!"

"Didn't I just see you yesterday?"

One night Clem's wife went into labor and the doctor was called to help with the delivery. Since there was no electricity, the doctor handed Clem a lantern and said, "Hold this high so I can see what I'm doing."

Before long a baby girl arrived.

"Wait a minute!" said the doctor. "Don't lower the lantern yet. I think there's another."

A moment later the doctor had delivered a second baby, this time a boy.

"Hold on!" cried the doctor a third time. "There's another one coming."

"Holy cow, Doc!" said Clem as he raised the lantern again. "Do you think it's the light that's attracting them?"

Doctor: Did you take my advice and sleep with the window open?

Woman: Yes, I did.

Doctor: Did you lose your cold?

Woman: No, but I lost my watch and handbag.

Nurse: Doctor, the man you just treated collapsed on the front step. What should I do?

Doctor: Turn him around so it looks like he was just arriving.

Why don't aardvarks get sick?

They are full of anti-bodies.

Doctor: Keep taking your medicine and you'll live to be a hundred.

Patient: Doc, I'll be a hundred next Wednesday.

Doctor: In that case, stop taking the medicine Thursday.

Sign at a false teeth clinic:

NOTHING DENTURED, NOTHING GAINED!!

When Luther came down with a bad case of the flu, he called his doctor for an appointment.

"The doctor can see you in three weeks," said the receptionist.

"Three weeks?" exclaimed Luther. "I might be dead in three weeks!"

"If that happens," replied the receptionist, "would you do us a favor and have someone call to cancel the appointment?"

How do ducks relieve pain?
Quackupuncture.

The absentminded professor arrived at the emergency ward with both of his ears badly burned.

"How did this happen?" asked the doctor.

"I was ironing my shirt," explained the professor, "when the phone rang and I answered the iron by mistake."

"What about the other ear?"

"That happened when I called for an ambulance."

❖

Patient: Doctor, I had a dream I ate a five-pound marshmallow and when I woke up, my pillow was missing.

Doctor: I find that hard to swallow.

Joe: Why is your doctor so dizzy?

Moe: Because he keeps making the rounds.

Patient: Doctor, I think I'm a mummy. What do you think?

Doctor: I don't think you're wrapped too tight.

Patient: How long do I have to live?

Doctor: I'd say about ten.

Patient: Years? Days?

Doctor: Nine . . . eight . . . seven . . . six . . .

Vinny went to his doctor to have his leg checked.

"My leg talks to me," said Vinny to the doctor. "If you don't believe me, just listen."

Vinny's doctor put his ear to the knee and heard a tiny voice say, "I need money."

"This is very serious," said Vinny's doctor.

He put his ear to the ankle and heard the tiny voice again. "I need money right now."

"What's wrong with my leg, Doc?"

"This is more serious than I thought," replied the doctor. "Your leg is broke in two places."

A man arrived at his doctor's office, anxious to hear the results of his hospital tests. "I have bad news and terrible news," said the doctor.

"The bad news is you have only 48 hours to live."

"What's the terrible news?"

"I left a message on your answering machine two days ago."

Patient: Doctor, how do I keep my ears from ringing?
Doctor: Get an unlisted head.

When the plumber arrived at Dr. Mackie's house, there was water all over the floor. Unpacking his tools, the plumber set to work on the broken pipe and within a few minutes handed the doctor a bill for $600.

"Six hundred dollars!" exclaimed the doctor. "This is ridiculous! I don't even make that much as a doctor."

"Neither did I when I was a doctor," smiled the plumber.

Doctor: How are those strength pills I gave you working?
Clem: I don't know. I'm not strong enough to get the cap off the bottle yet.

"Doctor, I'm here to be fitted for a hairpiece."

"Toupee?"

"Yes, of course, to pay, but I need the hairpiece first."

A man stubbed his toe so badly he decided to go to the doctor. When he arrived at the office, the nurse directed him to remove his clothes and wait in the next room.

"I just hurt my toe," complained the man. "Why do I need to take off my clothes?"

"Everyone who sees the doctor has to undress," explained the nurse. "It's our policy."

"Well, I think it's a stupid policy! Making me undress just to look at my toe!"

From the next room, another man's voice piped in, "That's nothing! I just came to fix the telephone."

Patient: Doctor, I think I'm a moth!
Doctor: How did you get in here?
Patient: Well, I saw this light in your window . . .

Patient: Doctor, I'm a burglar!
Doctor: Have you taken anything for it?
Patient: So far, I've taken two VCRs and a
DVD player.

Why is it that every time I go to the doctor, I feel like I'm on pins and needles?

A man rushed into an emergency room of a hospital and asked an intern for a cure for hiccups. Grabbing a cup of water, the intern quickly splashed it into the man's face.

"What did you do that for?" exclaimed the man.

"You don't have the hiccups now, do you?" said the intern.

"No," replied the man. "My wife out in the car has them."

Woman: My husband thinks he's a turtle.
Doctor: Have you tried talking to him?
Woman: It's no use—he won't come out of his shell.

Wife: Doctor, our marriage has never been the same ever since my husband started thinking he was a human boomerang.

Doctor: Don't worry, he'll come around.

"Doctor, Doctor, I think I'm a frog."

"Stick out your tongue."

"And say 'Ahh'?"

"No, I want you to get rid of that fly."

Dad: Hey, son, I heard you went out for the football team?

Chad: Yes. The coach sent me out to buy pizza.

What did the football coach say when he learned his piggy bank was stolen?

"I want my quarter back!"

What beverage helps boxers count?

A one-two punch.

❖

Two inexperienced hunters went hunting in the woods. Before long they got lost.

"Don't worry," said the first hunter. "I heard that when you're lost you should fire three shots in the air so somebody will hear you."

They fired three shots in the air and waited. A half hour later they tried again and still no one came. Finally they decided to try it a third time.

"This better work," said the second hunter nervously. "These're our last arrows."

A cricket walked into a London sporting goods store.

"Hey," said the clerk, surprised to see an insect with an interest in sports. "We have a game named after you."

"Really?" said the cricket modestly. "You have a game called Tyrone?"

Ed, Ned, and Fred went to the Summer Olympics but soon discovered that all the events were sold out. "I have an idea," said Ed. "Let's pose as athletes and they'll have to let us in."

The three agreed it was a good idea and Ed decided to go first. Running across the street to an old junk site he found a cast-iron roller. Lugging it in his hands he grunted and went past the security guard saying, "Williams, shotput," and was admitted.

Next, Ned ran to the same site and picked up a length of metal tubing. "Harris, pole vault," j173 he announced, and the guard waved him on.

Determined to follow his friends, Fred searched and searched the area until he discovered a roll of barbed wire. Striding up to the guard, he announced in a confident voice, "Johnson, fencing."

What famous baseball player always had
the sniffles?

Hankie Aaron.

What can you serve but never eat?

A volleyball.

What do you call a 100-year-old cheerleader?
Old Yeller.

What do acupuncture patients and bad wrestlers have in common?
Sooner or later, they all get pinned.

Why did the tennis coach give his team a lighter?
Because they kept losing their matches!

What do you call a basketball player who's always on the sidelines?
Hoop-less.

Duke: I'm taking a mail order weight-lifting class. Every week the postal carrier brings me a new set of weights.
Luke: Gee, you don't look you've gained any muscle.
Duke: No, but you should see the postal carrier.

How do they carry injured ballplayers off the field?
On the seventh-inning stretcher.

Did you hear about the track star who raced
a rabbit? He won by a hare.

Jerry: I just can't train my dog to hit home runs.
Terry: Why not?
Jerry: Because he prefers being walked.

Tom: Hey, Dad, I got good news and bad news. The good news is, my teammates elected me catcher.
Dad: What's the bad news?
Tom: The bad news is, I'm on the dart team.

How is losing money in a pay phone like a football game?

If you don't get the quarter back, you hit the receiver.

Clint: Do you know what I love best about baseball?
Flint: What?
Clint: The grass and the dirt, the lump in the throat.
Flint: Yeah, and that's just the hot dogs.

Larry: Can you spot me on the parallel bars?
Barry: Sure, you're right there.

"I bet I can run faster than you can," bragged Hank to his friend Bill one day.

"I bet you can't," replied Bill.

To prove his point, Hank took Bill to the roof of the tallest building in town, nearly 30 stories high. Hank removed his watch and, holding it over the edge of the building, let it drop. Quickly, in a whirl of dust, Hank dashed down the steps and, moments later, reaching ground level, held out his hand and caught the watch in it.

Signaling that it was his turn, Bill removed his watch and let it fall. Taking his time, he strolled to the elevator and pushed the button. A few minutes later the elevator appeared and, after stopping at several floors, finally arrived on the first floor. Stepping into the lobby, Bill stopped to get a soda from the vending machine, then calmly walked outside just in time for the watch to fall neatly into his hands

"Hey, that was amazing!" remarked Hank. "How did you do it?"

"Simple," said Bill. "My watch is five minutes slow."

Did you hear about the second-string football player who flooded the stadium with water? He was hoping the coach would send him in as a sub.

A horse walked up to the racetrack betting window and plunked his money down.

"I want to bet $50 on myself to win the fifth race," said the horse.

"I can't believe this!" said the astonished clerk.

"You can't believe what?" said the horse. "That I can actually talk?"

"No," replied the clerk. "I can't beleive you think you have a chance of winning the fifth race!"

"We'll never catch an elephant," sighed the first game hunter after a long day in the jungle. "Let's go home."

"I agree," replied the second. "Besides, I'm exhausted from carrying these decoys."

What happened to the baseball player who was always late for dinner?

His wife threw him out at home.

One day Milton asked his father to buy him a set of weight-lifting equipment. "I want to look like Arnold Schwarzenegger," said Milton. "Please?"

"All right," said Milton's father. "But you have to promise to use them every day."

That day at the sporting-goods store, Milton and his father picked out a set of weights and a bench press.

"Are you sure about this?" asked Milton's father.

"Please, Dad," said Milton. "I want to build up my muscles."

"Okay," said Milton's father when he had finished paying. "Let's get this home."

"You've got to be kidding, Dad," said Milton. "Do you expect me to carry this stuff to the car?"

Sign at fencing school:

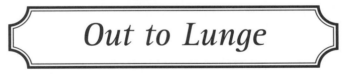

Out to Lunge

Two men at the racetrack were discussing their luck.

"An amazing thing happened to me the last time I was here," said the first man. "It was the ninth day of the month, and it was the day of my son's ninth birthday. The address of our house was 999, and I arrived here at the track at nine minutes past nine in the morning."

"I bet you put money on the ninth horse on the card," said the second man.

"Yes, I did," said the first man.

"And it won?"

"No, it came in ninth."

What baseball-playing spider has the highest batting average?

Ty Cobb-web.

One day a fisherman realized he had forgotten his bait. Spotting a frog with a worm in its mouth, he grabbed the frog and yanked the worm out. As a reward, he popped a candy bar into the frog's mouth.

A few minutes later, he felt a tug on his boot. When he looked down, he saw the same frog, but this time with three worms in its mouth.

Gert: The TV reception at our house is terrible.

Bert: How bad is it?

Gert: It's so bad, we get only two channels—on and off.

One night after his parents had gone to bed,
Freddy picked up the phone and dialed the
Psychic Hotline.

"Hello," said a woman's voice, "who's calling?"

"You're the psychic," said Freddy. "Why don't
you tell me?"

Lloyd: How did you enjoy that video about the pastry murderer?

Floyd: It was a real who-donut.

Why was Rip Van Winkle upset when he woke up?

His video rentals were overdue.

Mindy: Did you enjoy reading *The Pretzel Murders?*

Cindy: Yes, and I especially liked the twist ending.

Twelve-year-old Joey went to the movies. When he got there he saw a sign that said "Under 17 Not Admitted." So Joey went home and brought back 16 of his friends.

Why couldn't the crew play cards while waiting for the *Titanic* to sink?

Because the captain was standing on the deck.

Videos from the Nonfiction Shelf

Subtraction Magic
    hosted by Carry D. Wunn

How to Get Through School Faster
    hosted by Skip A. Yeer

Borrow and Get Rich Quick
    hosted by Allen U. Munny

Communicating with Porpoises
    hosted by Adolph Inne

Understanding Genetics
    hosted by Gene Poole

Better Home Security
    hosted by Eudora S. Open

The world's worst movie actor was giving a press conference after his latest premiere.

"Do you think you have improved as an actor?" asked one of the critics.

"Have you seen my last movie?" asked the actor excitedly.

"We hope so!" said the rest of the critics.

Lem: You're a promising singer.

Clem: Really?

Lem: Yes, in fact, you should promise to stop singing.

❖

"Daddy, will you buy me a bass drum?"

"No way, it's noisy enough around this house."

"But I promise to play it only when you're asleep."

❖

Little Henry got a cello and played it night and day. Unfortunately, every time he plucked a string, the family dog would whine and howl to no end.

Unable to stand the dog's suffering any longer, one day Henry's baby sister stormed into his room and pleaded, "For goodness' sake! Why don't you play something the dog doesn't know!"

Why is Elvis so cool?
Because of all his fans.

Two ants wandered inside a large-screen
television set. After crawling around for hours
the first ant started crying, "I think we're lost,
I think we're lost!"

"Don't worry, we'll get out," said the
second ant confidently. "I brought along a
TV Guide."

A boy was taken to the ballet by his mother. As the program began, the boy leaned over his seat and whispered, "Mom, they're all dancing on their toes."

"Yes, I know," shushed his mother. "That's the way they do it."

The boy watched for a moment longer and then said, "Well, why don't they just get taller dancers?"

Mindy: Did you enjoy the movie about the porcupine?
Cindy: Up to a point.

An oyster and a pig showed up to audition for a Broadway musical. As the director watched, the pig stepped onstage and broke into a terrible rendition of "Slop! In the Name of Love."
"No, no, sorry, next!" yelled the director.

Donning a top hat and tails, the oyster started tap-dancing, then finished by popping a pearl out of its shell. What do you think the director decided to do?

He cast pearl before swine.

What did the critics think of the cooking movie?

They gave it mixed reviews.

Moe: Did you hear there's a new movie about a convict who escapes from Alcatraz during a tornado?

Joe: What's it called?

Moe: *Con with the Wind.*

A man who had never been to the movies went to see his first film.

"I'll have one ticket, please," he said to the woman in the glass booth.

"But that's the third ticket you've bought in five minutes," said the ticketseller.

"I know," replied the man, "but before I get in the door some jerk keeps tearing them in half!"

What movie features two and a half hours of bugs hitting windshields?

Splat's Entertainment.

An Australian, a Canadian, and an American each bought a musical recliner. The next day, the Australian went back to the store and complained that when he sat down he sank too deeply into the cushion and had trouble getting up. Next, the Canadian returned his chair, saying that it was too slippery. Finally, the American arrived, asking for a refund.

"What's wrong?" asked the store manager, "is it too deep?"

"No, it's perfectly comfortable," said the American.

"Is it too slippery?"

"No, it feels just right."

"Then what is wrong with your musical recliner?"

"What's wrong? Every time I sit down, I hear 'The Star-Spangled Banner' and I have to stand up."

What movie features classical music and Dumbo dancing?

Ele-phantasia.

Zip: Did you hear about the new Broadway musical with the singing and dancing sardines?
Zap: I hear the show is really packing them in.

After the rock band had finished its audition, the record promoter scratched his head and said, "Your music's too loud, your lyrics are too crude, and the lead singer sounds like a cat screeching in a cactus patch."

"But what do you really think?" asked one of the band members.

"I think you'll sell a million," beamed the promoter, handing over the contract. "Sign here."

❖

The world's worst magician was on board the *Titanic*. One night, while performing in front of an audience he accidentally pulled a parrot out of a hat instead of a rabbit.

"You're a failure, you're a failure!" the parrot squawked.

Next, the magician tried levitating a woman, but the strings broke.

"You're a failure, you're a failure!" the parrot squawked again.

"For my next trick," said the magician, "I shall make this ship disappear."

Suddenly, at that very moment, the *Titanic* hit an iceberg and sank.

Later, when the parrot found itself clinging desperately to the magician aboard the lifeboat, the last of the ship disappeared beneath the ocean. "Sorry," squawked the parrot. "You're better than I thought you were."

Jeff: Do magicians do well on tests?
Steph: Yes, they're good at trick questions.

What did the compact disc player say to the CD?
   "Wanna go for a spin?"

How many mystery writers does it take to change a lightbulb?
   One, but he needs to give it a good twist.

Jill: What rating did the movie critics give *The Secret Garden*?

Phil: Two green thumbs up.

Dweebson thought he really was the world's smartest kid. Somehow, he actually ended up on a television quiz show.

"Okay, Dweebson," said the emcee. "Pick your subject."

"I'll take history for a million dollars," replied Dweebson.

"This is a two-part question," said the emcee. "Are you ready?"

"Yes," bragged Dweebson, "but I'm so smart, you can just ask me the second part."

"All right then, for a million dollars," said the emcee, "the second part of the question is— In what year did it happen?"

Why did the comb take acting lessons?
To get a good part.

Why did Lassie quit show business?
She was hounded by the press.

A Scotsman arrived in New York and soon was set up in his own apartment. After a few weeks, his mother called to see how he was doing.

"Terrible!" replied the Scotsman. "All day long some crazy guy bangs on my wall and yells, 'I can't take it anymore! I can't take it anymore!'"

"I'm so sorry," said his mother.

"But that's not all," said the Scotsman. "On the other side some woman cries and moans all day long."

"Well, Son," advised his mother, "if I were you, I'd keep to myself."

"Oh, I do," replied the Scotsman. "I just sit in my room all day and play the bagpipes."

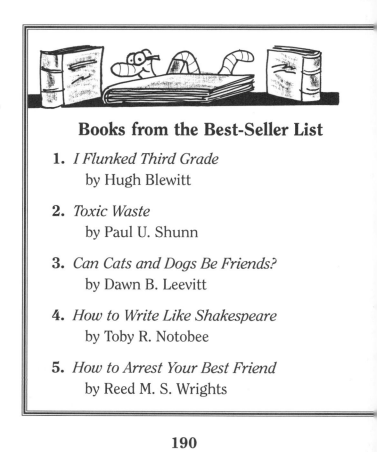

Books from the Best-Seller List

1. *I Flunked Third Grade*
   by Hugh Blewitt

2. *Toxic Waste*
   by Paul U. Shunn

3. *Can Cats and Dogs Be Friends?*
   by Dawn B. Leevitt

4. *How to Write Like Shakespeare*
   by Toby R. Notobee

5. *How to Arrest Your Best Friend*
   by Reed M. S. Wrights

Do cows like to sing?
Only country mooo-sic!

Derek: I bought a book called *How to Handle Disappointment.*
Eric: Was it helpful?
Derek: When I opened it, the pages were blank.

Best-Sellers from the DVD Shelf

Attack of the Flying Bloodsuckers
    starring Amos Quitoe

The Last Woman on Earth
    starring Emma Lone

Revenge of the Tiger
    starring Claude Body

Diary of a Mad Kidnapper
    starring Caesar Quick

My Three Years in Second Grade
    starring Dee Moted

Something Fishy
    starring Ann Chovie

What did the critics think of the gold rush movie?

They panned it.

Did you hear about the strongest man in the circus?

He could lift an elephant with one finger—but it took him ten years to find an elephant with one finger.

Jeff: Last night I came home to a family that gave me lots of love and sympathy.

Steph: That must have been nice.

Jeff: It was, except it was the wrong house.

Iggy: Hey, Ziggy, why are you so sad?

Ziggy: My sister said she wouldn't talk to me for 30 days.

Iggy: Why should that make you sad?

Ziggy: Today's her last day.

As she passed her son's room one night, Hank's mother heard a booming voice cry out, "To be or not to be! That is the question."

"Hank!" said his mother, knocking on the door. "What are you doing in there?"

"Exactly what you told me to," said Hank. "You said I should stay in my room until I learn how to act."

Will: Why are you grounded?

Bill: I tried to fill my father's shoes.

Will: Did you succeed?

Bill: Yes, I filled them with tacks.

Zack: My sister's on a raw-fish diet.

Jack: Has she lost any weight?

Zack: No, but she can balance a ball on her nose and bark like a seal.

Tim's absentminded father was reminiscing about his youth. "When I was your age," he said proudly, "I had to walk ten miles through the snow to get to school."

"Was it really that far?" asked Tim.

"Not really," said Tim's father, scratching his head. "It was right across the street, but I was terrible at directions."

Dill: Last night my sister and I had an argument, but it ended when she came crawling to me on her hands and knees.

Will: What did she say?

Dill: She said, "Come out from under that bed, you coward!"

Joe: My sister has a sun complex.

Moe: What's that?

Joe: She thinks that everything revolves around her.

Randy: My dad quit smoking cold turkey.
Sandy: How does he feel?
Randy: Better, but he's still coughing up the feathers.

Husband: Hey, honey, look at the new DVD player I got.

Wife: You know we can't afford a DVD.

Husband: Don't worry, I traded the TV for it.

❖

Two sisters came home from school crying their eyes out.

"What's wrong with you both?" asked their mother.

The first sister started wailing, "All the kids at school ever do is make fun of my big feet."

"There, there," soothed the mother. "Your feet aren't that big." She turned her attention to the second sister. "Now why are you crying?"

"Because I've been invited to a ski party," weeped the second sister, "and I can't find my skis."

"That's okay," said her mother, "you can borrow your sister's shoes."

❖

Bratty Clint and his sister went to the fair and found a nickel scale that tells your fortune and weight.

"Hey, listen to this," said Clint, showing his sister a small white card. "It says I'm bright, energetic, and a great brother."

"Yeah," Clint's sister said. "And it has your weight wrong, too."

A boy's father scolded him for breaking a neighbor's window with a baseball. "What did he say when you broke it?" asked the father.

"Do you want to hear what he said with or without the bad words?"

"Without, of course!"

"Well, then he said nothing."

Mom: Lenny, did you wake up grumpy this morning?

Lenny: No, I think Dad woke himself up.

Two toddlers went into their parents' bathroom and spotted their mother's scale in the corner.

"Whatever you, do," said the first tot to the second, "don't step on it."

"Why not?" asked the second.

"Because," replied the first, "every time Mom steps on it, she screams."

Once upon a time, there was a family that was so
cheap that everyone called them the
Cheapskates. They lived far away from their

nearest neighbors, and there weren't very many people or many businesses near them at all.

The Cheapskates had three sons. Their names were Cheap, Cheaper, and Cheapest.

One day, after pondering his future, Cheap decided to seek his fortune elsewhere, so he got up early the next day and left home.

Twenty years passed before Cheap returned home to visit his family. When he did, he was stunned to see his two brothers, Cheaper and Cheapest, had grown long beards that trailed all the way down to the floor.

Bewildered, Cheap asked them, "Why is your hair so long?"

"It's all your fault," replied Cheapest. "You took the razor."

❖

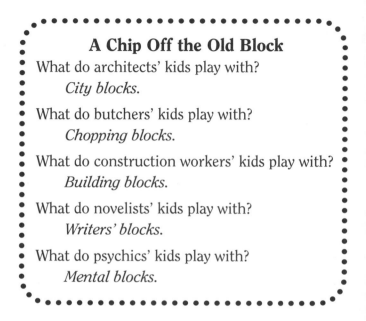

A Chip Off the Old Block

What do architects' kids play with?
City blocks.

What do butchers' kids play with?
Chopping blocks.

What do construction workers' kids play with?
Building blocks.

What do novelists' kids play with?
Writers' blocks.

What do psychics' kids play with?
Mental blocks.

When Oscar went away on vacation, his brother Harry promised to take care of his cat. The next day, Oscar called Harry to see how the animal was doing.

"Your cat is dead," said Harry, matter-of-factly.

"Dead?" said the shocked Oscar. "Why did you have to tell me like that?"

"How should I have told you?" asked Harry.

"Well," said Oscar, "the first time I called, you could have broken it to me gently. You could have said my cat was on the roof, but the fire department was getting her down. The second time I called, you could have told me the cat fell out of the fireman's arms and broke her neck. The third time I called, you could have said the vet did everything he could, but Fluffy passed away. That way it wouldn't have been so hard on me."

"I'm sorry," said Harry.

"That's all right. By the way, how's Mother?"

"She's up on the roof," said Harry, "but the fire department is getting her down."

WORK

What did one paleontologist say to the other?
"I have a bone to pick with you."

An astronaut graduated near the bottom of his class. On his first mission into space, he was teamed up with an orangutan. The astronaut and the orangutan were each given an envelope that they were to open once they got into space.

Moments after blastoff, the orangutan opened his envelope, read the contents, and then began flicking buttons and hitting switches.

Excitedly opening his envelope, the astronaut was surprised to discover three words of instruction:

"Feed the orangutan."

❖

Moe: My uncle's a farmer and a pool player.
Joe: I guess he has to mind his peas and cues.

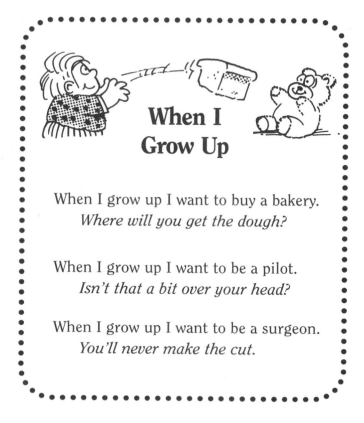

When I Grow Up

When I grow up I want to buy a bakery.
Where will you get the dough?

When I grow up I want to be a pilot.
Isn't that a bit over your head?

When I grow up I want to be a surgeon.
You'll never make the cut.

An astronaut in the space shuttle tried to take a picture of Earth from outer space, but it turned out blurry. Why?

Someone moved.

❖

Gene: What do overworked computer programmers do at the end of a long day?
Irene: They go home and crash.

A woman went to the zoo to apply for a job. When she arrived for the interview, the zookeeper told her he was looking for someone to dress up as a kangaroo to replace the real one that had been sent to another zoo.

"But I can't jump like a kangaroo," said the woman.

"Don't worry," the zookeeper reassured her. "We'll hide a trampoline behind some rocks and you can bounce up and down like the real thing."

The woman accepted and soon found herself in a kangaroo outfit leaping up and down on the trampoline. As the spectators cheered her, she got so caught up in the role that she bounced extra hard, then shot over the fence into the tiger's cage.

Scrambling to her feet, the woman began screaming hysterically, "Somebody help me! Help!"

The tiger inched closer and closer, then growled, "Shut up, lady, or we'll both lose our jobs."

Moe: What do an army private and a waitress have in common?
Joe: They both take orders all day long.

Vern: How was your first day at the lingerie shop?
Fern: I got the pink slip.

Hilarious Help-Wanteds

Barnyard Worker—guaranteed stable employment

Fisherman—must be willing to work for scale

Tuba Instructor—apply now and don't blow this opportunity

Driving Instructor—here's the brake you've been looking for

Part-Time Photographic—Assistant—may develop into full-time

214

The first day on the new job was a confusing one for Mr. Dithers. He stood in front of the huge piece of office equipment, trying to figure out all the buttons.

"Need some help?" offered one of the secretaries.

"Yes, how does this thing work?" asked Mr. Dithers, brandishing a thick pile of papers in his hands.

The secretary took the papers from him and began to feed them into the machine. Mr. Dithers watched in fascination as the machine tore each sheet into shreds.

"Thank you so much," said Mr. Dithers when the last paper had been shredded. "Now, where do the copies come out?"

What's the difference between a cattle herder and a locomotive driver?

One trains the steers, the other steers the trains.

Flip: After my uncle lost his job as a bus driver, he took up a life of crime.
Flop: How did he do?
Flip: He gave it up. Nobody would give him exact change.

Cindy: What do you get if you cross a leopard with a watchdog?
Mindy: A terified postman!

What's the difference between prospectors and butchers?

Prospectors stake their claims, butchers claim their steaks.

NOW HEAR THIS!

Did you hear about the moving-van driver who got carried away with his work?

A dweeb went to interview for a job. "What is two plus two?" asked the interviewer.

"Four," replied the dweeb.

"How do you spell 'cat'?"

"C-A-T," said the dweeb.

"What is your first name?"

"Wait a minute," said the dweeb. Then he began to sing, "Happy birthday to you, happy birthday to you . . ."

Why did the minister always videotape his sermons?

So he could watch them on instant repray.

Daffy Dan was out of work and needed money. He asked his best friend, Dudley, if there were any odd jobs he could do.

"As a matter of fact there are," said Dudley.

"Go into the garage, get a can of green paint and paint my porch."

A few hours later Dan knocked on Dudley's door.

"Well, it's done," Dan said, beaming proudly. "Except you were wrong about one thing. It's not a Porsche, it's a Ferrari."

Two hillbillies desperate for work went to the city to seek employment.

Spotting a sign with the words "Tree Fellers Wanted," the first hillbilly remarked to the second, "Too bad there's only two of us or we could have gotten a job."

Did you hear about the florist whose future looked rosy?

What was the first thing the lumberjack did when he bought a computer?

He logged on.

One day Iggy went for a walk and saw two men working in the park. The first man dug a hole, then the second man filled it up again with dirt. As Iggy watched, the men continued this same pattern all over the park. Finally, Iggy's curiosity got the best of him and he asked, "Why do you guys keep digging holes, then filling them back in?"

"It's real simple," said one of the workers. "There's usually a third guy who plants a tree, but he's out sick today."

Stanley got a job painting the yellow stripes

on the highway. His first day he dipped his brush into the bucket and managed to paint an entire mile of yellow lines. The second day he painted half a mile. The third day a quarter of a mile.

On the fourth day Stanley's boss showed up and asked, "How come each day you seem to paint less and less?"

"Well, sir," explained Stanley, "each day I get farther and farther away from the bucket."

A postal worker delivering a package knocked on the door of a house. A high-pitched voice said, "Come in."

Stepping inside, the postal worker suddenly found himself cornered by the biggest, most ferocious-looking dog he'd ever seen.

"Please!" called the postal worker. "Call off your dog!"

"Come in!" repeated the voice.

As the dog got closer and closer, its teeth bared and ready to pounce, the postal worker felt the sweat pouring off his brow. "Hey, lady, please call your dog off right now!" the postal worker repeated.

"Come in," said the voice again.

Finally, the postal worker crept into the living room with the dog still at his heels and saw

a parrot in a cage. "Come in!" squawked the parrot again.

"You stupid bird!" said the frightened postal worker. "Don't you know anything besides 'Come in'?"

"Squawk!" said the bird. "Sic him!"

Salesperson: I'm calling because our company replaced your windows with weathertight windows a year ago and we haven't received a single payment.

Customer: But you said the windows would pay for themselves in twelve months!

A dog went into the employment office and stepped up to the counter. "I need a job," said the dog.

"Well," said the clerk, astonished that the dog could talk, "with your rare talent, I'm sure we can get you something at the circus."

"The circus?" said the dog. "Why would the circus need a nuclear physicist?"

Salesman: Guess what, I got two orders today!
Boss: Congratulations! What were they?
Salesman: "Get out!" and "Stay out!"

You know it's going to be a bad day when
. . . all you get on Valentine's Day is a card
addressed "Occupant."

You know it's going to be a bad day when
. . . your alphabet soup spells out "Stupid."

You know it's going to be a bad day when
. . . you find out you're an underachiever and
your teacher is an overexpecter.

You know it's going to be a bad day when
. . . your VCR breaks down the same day you
win a video-club membership.

Leonard was not the brightest man in town, but when he heard the local sheriff was looking for a deputy, he decided he was right for the job.

"Before I hire you, I want you to answer some questions," said the sheriff. "What is 1 and 1?"

Thinking long and hard, Leonard finally answered, "11."

"Well, that's not what I meant," said the sheriff. "But I guess you're right. Okay, what two days of the week start with the letter *T*?"

"That would be today and tomorrow," said Leonard.

"Well, that's not what I meant, but I guess you're right. Now here's the last question—who killed Abraham Lincoln?"

"I don't know," said Leonard, looking confused.

"Well, why don't you go home and think about that one?"

That night Leonard went home and told his mother about the interview. "It went great," said Leonard excitedly. "First day on the job and already I'm working on a murder case!"

STUDENT RESPONSES

Teacher: Danny, when is the boiling point reached?
Danny: Usually when my father sees my report card.

Teacher: Name two ranges.
Class Clown: Gas and electric.

Teacher: Tony, please use the word *information* in a sentence.
Tony: Sometimes ducks fly information.

Teacher: Joey, if you're facing east, what would be on your right hand?
Joey: My fingers.

Teacher: Randy, did I catch you just now copying Alan's test paper?
Randy: No way, I haven't copied his paper for ten minutes.

Teacher: What do you want to get out of school the most?
Andy: Me.

Math Teacher: If I had 36 holes and filled in all but 9 holes, what would I have?
Harvey: A miniature golf course.

Teacher: What is aftermath?
Dana: The feeling you get when you finish an arithmetic test.

Teacher: Name the four food groups.
Stanley: Fast, canned, junk, and frozen.

Teacher: Manuel, define *ignorance* and *apathy*.
Manuel: I don't know and I don't care.
Teacher: Yes, that's correct.

Teacher: Vinny, your poem was the best in the class. Did you really write it?
Vinny: Yes, I wrote it while my mom dictated it.

Math Teacher: If there are a dozen flies on the table and you swat one, how many are left?
Math Clown: Uhhhh, just the dead one?

Teacher: Why did William Tell shoot an apple off his son's head?

Class Clown: Because he couldn't find an IBM.

Teacher: Billy, please use the word *arrest* in a sentence.

Billy: After pedaling up a steep hill on a bicycle, I sure need arrest.

Teacher: Sean, what is another name for a bunch of bees?

Sean: A good report card.

Teacher: It took close to one hundred years to build one pyramid

Class Clown: Must be the same contractor who's renovating our house.

Teacher: Use the word *apparent* in a sentence.

Clyde: When we come to Open School Night, we have to bring apparent.

Sunday School Teacher: Why did Moses wander in the desert for 40 years?

Sunday School Clown: He was too stubborn to stop and ask for directions?

Teacher: Janey, use the words *depart*, *decide*, and *deface* in a sentence.
Janey: Depart of your hair should never hang over decide of deface.

Teacher: When you finished your paper on the computer, did you do a grammar check?
Stacy: No, my grandma's usually in bed by seven.

Teacher: What kind of cat should you take into the desert?
Lem: A first aid kitty!

Teacher: If there are 365 days in the year, and 24 hours in a day, how many seconds are there?
Donald: Twelve.
Teacher: How do you figure that?
Donald: Well, there's January second, then February second, then March second . . . .

Science Teacher: What does your lab partner have in common with early apes?

Class Clown: Monkey breath?

Teacher: Lou, how many feet would you have if you combined an eight-foot snake with a five-foot snake?

Lou: None. Snakes don't have feet.

Teacher: The law of gravity explains why we stay on the ground.

Lester: How did we stay on the ground before the law was passed?

Teacher: Divide the circumference of a jack-o'-lantern by its diameter and what do you get?

Lefty: Pumpkin pi.

Teacher: Can you define *procrastination*?

Gomer: Yes, but not right now.

Teacher: What's a cat's favorite quote from Hamlet?

Janet: *"Tabby or not tabby!"*

Teacher: Bobby, have you lost your train of thought?

Bobby: No, but I think one of the cars just got derailed.

Teacher: Define absolute zero.
Henry: The lowest grade you can get on a test.

Teacher: Where is the Red Sea?
Howard: On the third line of my report card.

Teacher: Jerry, please use the word acquire in a sentence.

Jerry: Someday I want to sing in acquire.

Teacher: Why does the Statue of Liberty stand in New York Harbor?

Tim: Because the harbor is so crowded she can't sit down!

Teacher: How can you do so many stupid things in one day?

Andrew: I get up early.

Teacher: Joshua, if you worked nine hours a day for a dollar an hour, what would you get?

Joshua: A new job.

Teacher: What happens when salmon return to their place of birth?

Class Clown: All the other salmon sing "Happy Birthday"!

Teacher: Hank, please use the word *column* in a sentence.

Hank: When I want to talk to a friend, I column up on the phone.

First Aid Teacher: How do you call an ambulance?

Class Joker: "Hey, ambulance!"

Teacher: If you act up again, I'm going to teach you a thing or two!

Class Clown: Great! I'll double what I already know.

Sunday School Teacher: Do you want to go straight to heaven?

Sunday School Pupil: No, ma'am, my mother said I have to go straight home.

Teacher: Give an example of a national disaster.
Clown: How about my last report card?

Teacher: Why do cows eat green grass?
Shecky: Because they can't wait for it to ripen.

Teacher: If you misbehave again, I'll have to teach you a lesson.

Class Clown: Hooray, I'm finally going to learn something!

Teacher: If you ran 1,093 miles on Tuesday, then ran the same distance on Wednesday, what would you get?
Rama: Exhausted.

Teacher: Jack, please use the words head lice in a sentence.
Jack: When you drive at night, it's important to turn on your head lice.

Where's the rest of your homework?

I lost it fighting this kid who said you weren't the best teacher in school.

My friend fell into a clothes dryer. I jumped in to rescue him and my homework shrank.

I didn't want to add to your already heavy workload.

I hope it's not lost. I airmailed it to you late last night.

Rest of my homework? . . . That's not fair. I thought you said yesterday you were giving us a rest from homework.

Drat, those termites in my book bag are at it again!

I recycled it to save the environment.

Are your eyes on someone else's paper?

Oh, so that's where they landed!

Yes, but I was only checking for copyright violations.

Absolutely not—never once did my eyes leave my head.

Can't be mine. I always dot my eyes.

No, I was just testing my X-ray vision.

On the paper, no. On the ink, yes!

How do you think you'll ever get to high school with grades like this?

My stunning good looks, of course.

I try not to think—it gets in the way of my grades.

My uncle owns the bus company.

I'm hoping you'll be so sick of me you'll drive me over there yourself.

How did you manage to flunk every class?

I owe it all to that new program "Hooked on Stupidity."

Everyone needs a goal.

At least I'm consistent.

Practice makes perfect.

At least I didn't cheat!

I may flunked every class, but I had perfect attendance.

Not every class! I got an "A" in detention.

I didn't have time to do the homework until the ransom was paid.

Don't you like the food in the school cafeteria?

I like it at times—the times I see it swirling down the garbage disposal.

Are you kidding? The food's so bad even the teachers have food fights.

Is this a trick question?

From what I've heard, even the flies have to see the school nurse.

Interesting vocabulary choice. I wouldn't exactly call it food.

Yup, but I also like scratching my nails on a blackboard.

Maybe it was a typo, but I've been nervous ever since the menu read "Spit Pea Soup."

Yes, but I'm also fond of toxic waste.

Didn't I tell you to clean your room?

Yes, but I heard on the news that the president is going to be visiting disaster areas today.

Shh! I think Grandma is lost in my dirty laundry. Let's listen for tapping sounds.

I cleaned it, but my evil twin must have messed it up again.

I'm sorry, I think you have me confused with someone from a parallel universe.

I won't answer any more questions until my lawyer arrives.

Yes, but first you'll have to raise my allowance. Renting a bulldozer isn't cheap.

Do you think this is a hotel and I am your maid?

No, but you know those neat little soap bars—could you get me some of them?

Yes, and as a matter of fact, I wanted to talk to you about the lack of towels.

Of course not. By the way, what time is check-out?

Of course not. By the way, what time does the pool open?

Does this mean I don't have to tip you?

No, this is Buckingham Palace and you are my butler.

I'll call you later for room service.

Of course not. By the way, my wake-up call is 11 AM.

Actually, it feels more like Frankenstein's castle.

Is that your dog?

If he bites you he's not.

No, that's my pet ferret—he's going through an identity crisis.

No, my cat always dresses up for Halloween.

No, that's my dad. I was raised by wolves.

No, it's a giant hairball with legs.

No, my sister's a witch and that's what's left of her new boyfriend.

Shh! Not too loud—he thinks he's the world's smartest hamster.

Why should I increase your allowance?

I'm saving up for a beach house.

My piggy bank went bankrupt.

What allowance? I can't even afford to pay anyone a compliment.

Then you won't have to worry about me digging under the sofa cushions when you're trying to take a nap.

Did you cut your finger?

Yes, I'm trying to trap a vampire.

Ever hear of DNA? It stands for "Do Not Ask"!

No, but I have a whole box of Band-Aids that are about to expire and I have to use them up.

No, my finger prefers to cut itself, thank you.

No, it's ketchup just in case I'm attacked by a French fry.

No, I'm really an alien invader and I use this red stuff to mark my territory.

Yes, I'm auditioning for a part in the new reality series: "World's Worst Paper Cuts."

No, it's just a simple computer byte.

Is it true your parents grounded you?

No, it's false. The FBI has me under house arrest.

My astrologer told me not to go out until New Year's.

Yes, cut off from everything with only my CDs, DVDs, TV, PC, and cell phone to keep me company.

No, that's an out-and-out lie and as soon as I'm allowed to leave my house, I'll set the record straight.

Not really, they just want me home more to talk to the houseplants.

Nonsense, I can go anywhere I want—like the living room, den, kitchen . . . even the garage.

Grounded? No. It's more like my house is an airport and I've only gotten clearance to taxi to the end of the driveway.

Are you doing your homework right now?

I'm doing my homework. Whether it's right or not is up for debate.

No, I thought I'd do someone else's homework.

No, I'm doing it last week. You just traveled back in time.

No, I'm writing a story about someone who always asks stupid questions and ends up turning into a toad.

No, I'm adding up how many times a minute you interrupt me.

Are you waiting to use the bathroom?

No, I'm from the census bureau. I'm counting toilets.

No, I'm practicing for my dance recital.

No, I'm modeling my underwear for all the world to see.

No, I'm waiting for you to use the bathroom so I can sneak into your room and short-sheet your bed.

No, I'm a lost rock 'n' roll star waiting for my tour bus to arrive.

Bathroom! I thought it was the batroom. No wonder Bruce Wayne hasn't arrived.

Did you lose a tooth?

No, I'm just renting it out.

No, I got tired of brushing it so I sent it out
to be cleaned.

No, it had a fight with my tongue and moved out.

No, my dentist is just borrowing it for a necklace.

No, I'm remodeling my mouth. Look—I gained a
space to put in a straw.

No, it's on an amusement park field trip riding the
molar coaster.

No, it's out partying—having a rootin'-tootin'
good time.

Are you going fishing?

No, I'm taking my pet worms to a splash party.

No, I'm using this device to eavesdrop on submarine conversations.

No, I've been hired by SeaWorld to floss Shamu's teeth.

Do you call this a book report?

No, I called it quits after I fell asleep.

No, I call it Spot, but it doesn't seem to respond.

No, I call it a doorstop—you can call it what you want.

I'm sorry, I'm beyond the name—calling stage.

No, you can use it as a paper hat, or as a sailboat.

The Web site I copied it from claimed it was.

No, I see it as more of a cry for help.

No, I see it as a first draft with big expectations.

No, I call it a "Cook Report," because it's really only half-baked.

No, I call it my ticket to detention.

No, I call a colossal waste of paper.

Is it raining out?

No, I just wanted to make a big splash.

No, my armpits are on overdrive.

No, that wacky school janitor accidentally
hooked the water fountain up to the fire
hose again.

No, I decided to take a shower in my clothes.

No, I always sweat on my way to school.

No, I got caught in the crossfire of a spitball fight.

No, I think there's a problem with the second-
floor sink.

No, my mom forgot to close my window at the
car wash.

No, this is part of my show-and-tell exhibit on soggy shorts.

No, I'm working part-time as a lawn sprinkler installer.

271

Haven't you gotten out of bed yet?

Yes, and it was so tiring I got right back in.

What for? Tomorrow morning you'll just ask me to get out all over again.

I did that yesterday and didn't like the results.

No, because tonight you'll just be yelling for me to go to bed.

Are you taking a bath?

Yes, I think I'll take it to the movies.

No, I'm reenacting the final scene from *Titanic*.

No, I'm practicing synchronized swimming for the Olympics.

No, I'm exercising my rubber ducky.

No, the girls all say I look cute in dirt.

No, I'm just studying for my plumber's final exam.

No, but if I stay in here another hour I'll have enough wrinkles to be a raisin for Halloween.

You aren't afraid of shots, are you?

Well, when you said, "Get a booster," I thought you meant a higher cushion.

Ghosts, zombies, mummies, no. Shots, yes.

It depends on who's calling them.

I don't mind the shots, but the sight of cotton balls makes me faint.

Reassuring voice of an airplane pilot:

"This is your captain speaking. I have good news and bad news. The bad news is we have just run out of fuel. However, the good news is I'm parachuting down to get help."

A farmer went to a fair. He jumped for joy when he saw they had old-fashioned airplane rides. The problem was, he didn't want to pay $25 for one ride.

"Tell you what I'll do," said the pilot. "If you can fly with me and not say a single word, I'll give you every cent in my pocket. Otherwise, you pay full price." The farmer agreed and before long they were up in the sky, flying upside down and weaving through the clouds in every direction.

When they landed, the pilot shook the farmer's hand in amazement. "You didn't speak a single word. How did you do it?"

"It was sure tough," replied the farmer. "Especially when your wallet slipped out of your pocket."

How do you launch a kitten?
With a cater-pillow!

Did you hear about the dweeb who kept a stick of dynamite in his car's emergency repair kit? He figured if he got a flat he could blow up his tires.

A helicopter pilot running out of gas soon found himself in the middle of the desert. Spotting a group of hikers, he quickly made a sign saying "Where am I?" Hovering over them, the pilot put the sign to the window so they could see it.

Conversing for a few minutes, the hikers soon made their own sign and flashed it at the helicopter pilot. Their sign said, "You're in a helicopter."

❖

Seymour was riding his new bike down the street when he knocked over an old woman.

"You stupid, idiotic boy!" fumed the woman as she struggled to her feet. "Don't you know how to ride a bike?"

"Of course I do," replied Seymour. "I just don't know how to ring the bell."

Gene: What type of automobile would an elephant drive?
Irene: I don't know, but I bet it would have to have plenty of trunk space.

Sign at a car dealership: "The Best Way to Get Back on Your Feet—Miss a Car Payment."

Police Officer: Can you explain why you were driving on the wrong side of the road?
Out-of-Towners: I certainly can. The other side was full.

A woman got on a bus but soon regretted it. The driver sped down the street, zigzagging across the lanes, breaking nearly every rule of the road.

Unable to take it any longer, the woman stepped forward, her voice shaking as she spoke. "I'm so afraid of riding with you, I don't know what to do."

"Do what I do," said the bus driver. "Close your eyes."

Lenny: According to motor vehicle statistics, a man gets hit by a car every 38 minutes.
Benny: If I were him, I'd stay off the street!

Where do old car tires end up?
On skid row.

A tourist driving down a deserted road came face to face with a sign that said "Road Closed. Do Not Enter." As the road ahead looked pretty good, he ignored the sign and drove on.

A few miles later he came to a bridge that was down. He promptly turned around and retraced his route. As he reached the point where the warning sign stood, he read the words on the other side: "Welcome Back, Stupid!"

What has 100 legs and goes, "Ho-Ho-Ho!"
Santa-pede.

When their car broke down in the desert, Larry, Harry, and Carey decided to go their separate ways for help.

Larry took the radiator out of the car so he could have water for his journey. Harry took the hubcaps off so he could use them to shield his

face from the sun. Carey, however, removed the door and started off down the road.

"Wait a minute," said Larry. "Why are you taking the door with you?"

"In case I need some air," replied Carey. "I can roll the window down."

Student Driver: How did I do squeezing into that space?

Driving Instructor: Not bad. But next time try parking on top of a sturdier car.

❖

The man pulled over to the side of the road when he heard the police siren.

"How long have you been riding around without a taillight?" asked the officer.

"Oh, no!" screamed the man, jumping out and dashing to the rear of the car.

"Calm down," said the officer. "It isn't that serious."

"Wait'll my family finds out."

"Where's your family?"

"They're in the trailer that was hitched to the car!"

Tip: I've started keeping my bicycle in my bedroom.
Top: Why are you doing that?
Tip: I got tired of walking in my sleep.

Emma: My teacher was in a car accident.
Gemma: What happened?
Emma: She was grading papers on a curve.

How Do They Travel?

Frogs hop a plane.

Hens fly the coop.

Snakes slide home.

Kangaroos jump ship.

286

A man drove his car into the middle of a tornado and soon found himself spinning out of control. Before he knew it his car was dangling halfway over the edge of a cliff. Quickly, he dialed the police on his cell phone and shouted, "Help! I'm caught in the storm."

"Don't worry," the dispatcher assured him. "It'll blow over."

"That's exactly what I'm afraid of," wailed the man.

Mr. Dithers knew he was late when he spotted the ferry just a few feet from the dock. Running as fast as he could, he leaped across the water, barely landing on the boat's deck.

"That was sure close," said Mr. Dithers as a nearby stranger helped him to his feet.

"What's the hurry?" said the stranger. "This ferry's just arriving."

Did you hear about the silly man who drove his truck off the cliff? He wanted to test his new air brakes.

A truck driver named Horace was driving along the freeway when he saw a sign, "Low Bridge Ahead." Thinking his truck could easily make it, Horace drove under the bridge and got stuck. Soon the other cars were honking their horns and shouting at Horace. Before long, a police officer arrived and smiled at Horace's predicament.

"Well, what's the problem? A little stuck, huh?" said the officer.

Thinking quickly, Horace grinned and replied, "No, I didn't get stuck. I was delivering this bridge and ran out of gas."

Nutty New Airlines

Donut Airlines—We fly circles around everyone else.

DNA Airlines—We never leave you stranded.

Dental Airlines—We pull out all the stops for you.

King Oscar Airlines—We pack you in like sardines.

Chaplain's Choice Airlines—We get you there on a wing and a prayer.

Why did the robber steal a crate of fat ducks?
He heard they had big bills.

Refusing to surrender his money to a mugger, Mr. Cummings put up a fight. After a long struggle, the mugger finally overcame Mr. Cummings to discover only 57 cents in his pocket.

"You put up a fight like that for a lousy 57 cents?" said the mugger.

"I'm sorry," said Mr. Cummings. "I thought you were after the 400 dollars I hid in my shoe."

Warden to death-row prisoner:
"Any last requests?"
"Yes, I'd like a cigarette."
"Are you crazy? That stuff'll kill you!"

Why would Snow White make a great judge?
Because she's the fairest of them all.

Vern: Did you hear about the depressed prisoner?

Fern: What was his problem?

Vern: He was down, but not out.

Judge: Why do you always rob the same store?
Crook: Because the sign on the door says "Please Come Back Soon."

Why was the Tupperware salesman ruled out as a murder suspect?
He had an airtight alibi.

❖

Molly: The crime in my neighborhood is really bad.
Polly: How bad is it?
Molly: It's so bad, the other night I forgot my key to the house and the burglar had to let me in.

Why was the dishwasher arrested?
For panhandling.

Prisoner to new cellmate:

"What are you in for?"

"Driving too slow."

"You mean too fast?"

"No, too slow. If I had been driving faster, they wouldn't have caught me."

From the Prison Video Library

Prison Break
starring Doug A. Tunnel

Life Sentence
starring Noah Parole

Judge: You are accused of stealing garments from the clothesline of a convent. What do you have to say for yourself?

Crook: I promise I won't make a habit of it.

The warden of the prison felt sorry for one of his inmates. Every weekend, while most of the prisoners were visited by family and friends, poor George sat alone in his cell.

One visiting day the warden called George into his office. "I notice you never have any visitors, George," said the warden, putting a comforting hand on George's shoulder. "Tell me, don't you have any friends or family?"

"Oh, sure I do, Warden," replied George cheerfully. "But they're all in here."

Traffic Cop: Why didn't you stop when I blew my whistle?

Driver: I'm a little deaf.

Traffic Cop: Don't worry, you'll get your hearing tomorrow.

A police officer pulled a man over for speeding. Thinking quickly, the man said to the officer, "It's an emergency. My mother's in the backseat. She took an overdose of reducing pills."

Checking the backseat, the officer shook his head. "I don't see anyone back there."

"Oh, no!" cried the man. "I'm too late!"

Tutti: What would you do if you crossed an umpire with a burglar?

Frutti: Someone who breaks into your home and yells "safe!"

What do you call a bug that arrests other bugs?
A cop-roach.

What game do gangsters play?
Racket-ball.

A police officer was escorting a prisoner to jail when his hat blew off down the sidewalk.

"Shall I run and get it for you?" said the prisoner.

"You must think I'm really stupid!" said the officer. "You wait here and I'll get it."

Police Chief: Keep an eye on the beach. We've had reports of someone stealing surfboards.
Officer: Wow, Chief, sounds like a crime wave.

Gert: Which color isn't afraid to take a lie detector test?
Bert: True blue.

Police Examiner: If you were by yourself in a police car and were pursued by a gang of criminals in another car doing 60 miles an hour, what would you do?
Police Candidate: Seventy.

Kenny: My parents just installed a brand-new home security system. We have steel bars on the windows, five locks on the door, and an electrified fence outside.

Lenny: Boy, I bet you'll never get robbed.

Kenny: Robbed? I can't even get out of my own house.

The judge shook his head sadly when the prisoner appeared in his courtroom.

"The first time you were arrested for burglary, the second time for stealing a car, and the third time for mugging someone. What do you have to say for yourself?"

"Well, Your Honor," replied the crook, "I guess it takes some folks longer than others to find out what they're good at."

Why did police think Bo Peep was involved in the big sheep robbery?

She'd been seen with a crook!

Officer: You can't park there!
Driver: Why not? The sign says "Fine for Parking."

Homer: Why are bananas lawyers' favorite fruit?
Gomer: Because they like a-peels.

The boss of a big burglary operation was breaking in a new thief.

"Tonight, we're going to rob the lingerie company," said the boss to the rookie. "And remember—this time no slips."

❖

Trixie: Is it true your mom drives too fast?
Dixie: Are you kidding? She got stopped for speeding so many times the police gave her season tickets.

Zip: The world's dumbest robber broke into our house and stole the TV remote control.
Zap: So what's so bad about that?
Zip: Every time he passes our house he changes channels.

Motorcycle Cop: Sir, were you in high gear when you had the accident?
Silly Driver: No, I was in my tennis gear.

Did you hear about the dumbest robber in the world? He waved his gun at the bank teller and said, "Give me $10,000," then went to the next window to open an account.

Joe: My brother is connected to the police department.
Moe: In what way is he connected?
Joe: By a pair of handcuffs.

Harry: My uncle's with the FBI.
Larry: Is that so?
Harry: Yes, they picked him up trying to leave the country.

Willie: My uncle started out life as an unwanted child.

Dillie: Have things changed?

Willie: You bet. Now he's wanted in fifty states.

305

Hilarious Headlines

**"Police Are Campaigning to
Run Down Jaywalkers"**

"Police Crack Down on Egg Robbers"

**"Boy Struck by Lightning
Faces Battery Charge"**

"Woman Steals Clock, Faces Time"

One day Howard was driving to the lake for a swim when he noticed a man on the side of the highway dressed all in red.

"Who are you?" asked Howard as he pulled up to the stranger.

"I'm the Man in Red and I'm very hungry," said the man.

Reaching into his lunch sack, Howard pulled out a sandwich, handed it to the man, then sped off down the road.

A few miles later, Howard spotted another man, this time dressed all in yellow.

"What can I do for you?" asked Howard.

"I'm the Man in Yellow and I'm very thirsty."

Howard pulled out a can of soda, handed it to the man, then resumed his journey.

Anxious to get to the lake before sunset, Howard put his foot to the pedal and roared off down the road, only to spot yet another man, dressed all in blue, signaling for Howard to stop.

"Don't tell me!" said Howard impatiently. "You're the Man in Blue, right?"

"That's right!" replied the man.

"Well, what do you want?"

"Driver's license and registration, please."

Why were the police called when the chicken failed to cross the road?

Fowl play was suspected.

A burglar broke into a house and stole a man's money and dentures. When he was arrested, the police gave him a polygraph test and found he was lying through someone else's teeth.

"Your Honor," said the smartest lawyer in the world, "my client is not guilty. He merely inserted his arm into a window and stole some jewelry. His arm is not himself. I fail to see how you can punish the whole individual for an offense committed by one arm."

"I agree," nodded the judge. "I hereby sentence the defendant's arm to one year in prison. He may accompany the arm or not."

"Thank you, Your Honor," said the defendant as he detached his artificial limb, laid it on the bench, and walked out.

The private detective had just moved into his new office when he heard a knock at the door. Hoping to make a good impression on his first customer, he yelled, "Come in!" and then picked up the telephone and pretended he was talking to someone important.

The visitor waited patiently. Finally, the detective hung up the phone and said, "As you can see, I'm very busy. What can I do for you?"

"Not much," said the man. "I'm here to hook up your phone.

❖

Silly Prisoner #1: I hear you're in prison because you're a sentimental guy.

Silly Prisoner #2: That's right. I put my mother's picture on the 20-dollar bills I was making.

Lem: What happens to cats when they get out of prison?
Clem: They go on purr-ole.

The police officer arrived at the scene of a grocery-store holdup and said to the clerk who had been robbed, "You say the suspect helped himself to three bags of pretzels, the cash register, and a pair of pants?"

"That's right; officer," said the clerk.

"I'm glad you didn't chase after him," said the officer.

"How could I?" replied the clerk. "They were my pants!"

Nit: Why do cats chase birds?
Wit: For a lark!

How do you tell the difference between a bad undercover cop and a good boxer?

One blows his cover, the other covers his blows.

Did you hear the one about the cowboy who put superglue on his six-shooters? He always stuck to his guns.

Did you hear about the crook who tried to hold up a busload of tourists? The police have 2,000 photographs of the suspect.

What kind of dog wears jeans and a T-shirt and fights crime?

A plainclothes police dog!

A crook rushed into a library and pointed a gun at the clerk.

"This is a stickup!" said the crook.

"Can't you see that sign?" said the librarian in a whisper. "It says 'No Loud Noises in the library.'"

"Don't worry, "the crook reassured her, "I'm using a silencer."

❖

When Mr. Bumble saw an ad in the paper that said, "Pedigreed police dog for sale, $40," he went to the pet store and plunked his money on the counter.

A few moments later the owner brought out the mangiest-looking dog Mr. Bumble had ever seen.

"You call this a pedigreed police dog?" huffed Mr. Bumble angrily.

"Don't be fooled by his looks," reassured the owner. "He's really in the Secret Service."

Policeman: Your driver's license says you should be wearing glasses.

Motorist: I have contacts.

Policeman: I don't care whom you know, you're still getting a ticket.

Two horse thieves were arrested by a posse of cowboys, who decided to hang them for their crimes. Unable to find any trees, the cowboys took the rustlers to a bridge and tied a rope around the first man's neck. Unfortunately, the rope broke and the thief fell into the river and swam off to safety.

As they tightened the noose around the second man's neck, he managed to stammer, "I sure hope this is a strong rope."

"Why's that?" asked one of the cowboys.

"Because," gulped the thief, "I can't swim."

Dilly: What happened to Frankenstein when he was caught speeding?
Dally: He was fined $50 and dismantled for six months.

Dad: Well, Todd, now that we got you a waterbed, are you still afraid of monsters?

Todd: No, now I'm afraid of sharks.

Chad: Hey, Dad, look at this great watch I found in the street.

Dad: Are you sure it was lost?

Chad: Of course it was lost. I saw the guy looking for it.

Little Sara found a jigsaw puzzle and worked on it every night for two weeks until it was finished.

"Look what I did!" she said, showing off the puzzle to her best friend.

"Wow, how long did it take you?" asked her friend.

"Two weeks—can you believe it?"

"You call that fast?" said her friend, unimpressed.

"You bet it is," replied Sara, showing her friend the puzzle box. "Look—it says 'From Two to Four Years.'"

What did the DVD say to the radio?
"You just don't get the picture, do you?"

"Why did you cut a big hole in your umbrella?"
"So I can see when it stops raining."

Two boys were camping in the backyard. When they couldn't figure out what time it was, the first boy said to the second, "Start singing very loud."

"How will that help?" said the second boy.

"Just do it," insisted the first.

Both boys broke into song, singing at the top of their lungs. Moments later, a neighbor threw open her window and shouted, "Keep it down! Don't you know it's three o'clock in the morning?"

Barber: Your hair needs cutting badly.

Customer: No, it needs cutting nicely. You cut it badly last time.

Will: What do you call a kid with a lightbulb in his head?
Dill: Pretty bright.

What's a good remedy for squeaky infants?
Baby oil.

Once upon a time there lived a prince who was under the spell of an evil witch. The prince could speak only one word per year. However, he could save up words so that after two years he could speak two words, and after three years he could speak three words, and so on.

One day the prince met a beautiful princess and fell madly in love with her. He decided to ask the princess to marry him. Realizing he was still under the witch's curse, the prince waited and saved up a word each year for nine long years. When the fateful day arrived, the prince got down on his knee and said, "My Darling, I love you! Will you marry me?"

To which the princess replied, "I'm sorry, I wasn't paying attention. What did you say?"

Did you hear about the guy who's so lazy he hires other people to walk in his sleep?

Clara: I read this pamphlet that said "By the time you finish reading this paragraph, someone will have died."
Sara: What did you do?
Clara: I stopped reading right away.

Mr. Winterbottom arrived at the airport and spotted a computerized scale in the lobby. Curious, he dropped a quarter in the slot and stepped on it as a voice announced, "You are five feet, ten inches tall, weigh 165 pounds, and you are taking a plane to Australia."

Impressed by the machine's accuracy, he tried it again. "You are five feet, ten inches tall," the voice repeated, "weigh 165 pounds, and you are taking a plane to Australia."

The third time he decided to try to fool the machine. He took his suitcase into the men's room and changed into a different coat and tie. Pulling his hat over his ears to hide his face, Winterbottom dropped another quarter into the machine. "You are five feet, ten inches tall, weigh 165 pounds," the voice announced, then added, "and while you were changing your clothes, you missed the plane to Australia."

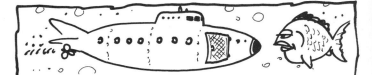

World's Dumbest Inventions

The waterproof towel

Glow-in-the-dark sunglasses

Inflatable dartboards

Solar-powered flashlights

Waterproof tea bags

Powdered water

Submarine screen doors

The cordless extension cord

Plumber to woman:

"Okay, where's the drip?"

"He's in the bathroom trying to fix
the leak."

Did you hear about the new Divorced Barbie?
It comes with half of everything Ken owns.

Bert: I bought a lousy AM radio.
Gert: AM? Why didn't you buy one you could
play at night, too?

❖

What has a nice trunk but never goes on
a trip?
A tree.

On Halloween three boys went to a *Star Trek* costume party. The first boy walked through the door wearing pointed ears and arched eyebrows. The host of the party looked at him and said, "What have you come as?"

"Isn't it logical?" replied the boy. "I'm Mr. Spock."

The second boy entered wearing black boots, black pants, and a red sweater.

"And what have you come as?" said the host.

"Aye, can't you see?" replied the second boy. "I'm Scotty, the engineer."

Finally, a third boy stepped forward dressed in the shape of a tree.

The host looked baffled and asked, "And what are you?"

"Isn't it obvious?" snapped the boy. "I'm the captain's log!"

Harry: Did you hear about the boatload of shoes that sank in the Atlantic?

Larry: No, what happened?

Harry: Three hundred soles were lost at sea.

Dan: Why did Arthur have a Round Table?
Fran: So no one could corner him!

Willy: What do you get when you cross track shoes with comedy?
Billy: A running joke.

A man missed his bus and decided to walk home. He had journeyed several miles when night began to fall. Stumbling exhausted into a cemetery, the man laid down on the grass, rolled over, then slid into an open grave.

The next morning, an old woman arrived at the cemetery and, just as she approached the gravesite, she heard a voice murmur, "I'm so cold!"

Staring down into the grave, she replied, "Well, no wonder, you poor thing. You kicked all your dirt off."

Morris: What does Superman hate most about the new phone technology?
Boris: Did you ever try changing into blue tights and a cape behind a cell phone?

Just in the nick of time the fire department arrived at a house engulfed in flames.

Rushing inside, one of the firemen pulled an absentminded professor from his bed and led him safely outside.

"That oughta teach you to smoke in bed!" said the fireman to the professor.

"Who was smoking?" coughed the professor.

"That bed was on fire when I got into it."

❖

"Waiter!" snapped the angry customer as the sweat poured off his face. "It's hot in here. Turn up the air conditioner."

"Whatever you say," replied the waiter.

"Waiter!" yelled the customer a few minutes later, shivering. "It's too cold in here. Turn the air conditioner down."

"Whatever you say, sir," said the waiter.

"Say, waiter," said another customer nearby. "Why don't you ask that pest to leave?"

"Oh, he doesn't bother me," said the waiter. "We don't have an air conditioner."

What has no fingers but many rings?
A tree.

Iiggy: What is the height of stupidity?
Ziggy: I don't know, how tall are you?

Irving was walking past a department store when he saw a handsome-looking suit in the window.

"May I try on that suit in the window?" he asked one of the store clerks.

"No, I'm sorry," replied the clerk, "you'll have to use the dressing room like everyone else."

A hunter got lost in the woods. After wandering in the forest for three days, exhausted and starving, he spotted a forest ranger coming toward him.

"Thank goodness you found me!" said the relieved hunter. "I've been lost for three days!"

"You think that's bad?" replied the ranger. "I've been lost for two weeks."

What do you call people who watch other people diet?

Weight Watchers.

Dill: I hooked my microwave to my computer.

Will: Why did you do that?

Dill: Now I can get my homework done in half the time.

Three men stranded on a tropical island came upon a lamp buried in the sand. They rubbed the lamp and a genie appeared in a puff of smoke.

"I'll grant you three wishes," said the genie.

"I wish I was home with my family," said the first man. The genie waved his hand and POOF! The first man vanished in a puff of smoke.

"I wish I was back home with my friends," said the second man and POOF! He too disappeared in a cloud of smoke.

The third man thought long and hard until the genie tapped his fingers impatiently and snapped, "What is it you wish?"

The third man sniffled and said, "I wish my two friends were back to keep me company."

Why did the computer go to the eye doctor?
  To improve its Web-sight.

Molly: Would you say I'm a person of rare
intelligence?
Dolly: Yes, it's rare when you show any.

As he checked out of the Slowpoke Hotel, the man suddenly realized he had forgotten his luggage. Turning to the bellhop, he shouted, "Run up to room 843 and see if I left my suitcase there."

"Sure thing," drawled the bellhop, who started moving slowly toward the elevator.

"Hurry!" the man pleaded. "My plane leaves in ten minutes."

"Whatever you say," said the bellhop, then he disappeared.

Five minutes later the clerk returned, out of breath and empty-handed.

"Well?" said the man desperately. "Did I leave my suitcase there?"

"Yep," replied the bellhop happily. "You left it on the bed."

One day Hubert discovered a bottle buried in the sand. When he rubbed it, a genie appeared and said, "I grant you three wishes."

"I want to be the richest man on earth," said Hubert.

A puff of smoke rose in the air and soon the entire beach was covered with millions of gold coins!

"Next," said Hubert thoughtfully, "I want a body just like Arnold Schwarzenegger's."

Another puff of smoke and suddenly Hubert had the finest muscles ever seen on a man.

"Finally," Hubert smiled, "for my last wish I want to be irresistible to girls."

One final puff of smoke and zap! Hubert turned into a Barbie doll.

❖

Three mice were bragging about which of them was the toughest. "I'm so tough I once ate a whole bag of rodent poison and lived to tell about it."

"Oh yeah?" scoffed the second mouse. "I'm so tough I was caught in a mouse trap and bit it apart!"

"See you later!" said the third mouse as he scurried off.

"Where are you going" asked the other two mice. I'm off to harass the cat," replied the third.

341

As the storm began to rage, the absentminded professor started outside when his wife stopped him, asking, "Where do you think you're going?"

"I'm going out to water the flowers," replied the professor.

"But it's raining outside!" said his wife.

"You're right," said the professor, closing the door and walking to the closet. "I'd better take my umbrella."

❖

Lem: My town is so small our fire department has a hose, a cart, and four dogs.
Clem: What are the dogs for?
Lem: They know where to find the hydrant.

Why did the bungee jumper take a vacation?
Because he was at the end of his rope.

What did the computer say when the little lamb logged on?

"Ewe got mail."

Two absent-minded professors were watching TV one night. "How about a dish of ice cream?" said the first professor.

"Sounds good." replied the second professor.

"I'll write it down so you won't forget."

"Don't worry, I won't forget," replied the first professor.

"But I want chocolate syrup and nuts on it."

"How could I forget that?"

A few minutes later the first professor returned with a plate of bacon and eggs.

"See I knew I should have written it down," said the second professor. You forgot the buttered toast."

Index